Advisory Board

The ASHE Higher Education Report Series is sponsored by the Association for the Study of Higher Education (ASHE), which provides an editorial advisory board of ASHE members.

D1400309

ASHE Higher Education Report: Volume 33, Number 1
Kelly Ward, Lisa E. Wolf-Wendel, Series Editors

Are the Walls Really Down? Behavioral and Organizational Barriers to Faculty and Staff

Alvin Evans
Edna Breinig Chun

Are the Walls Really Down?
Behavioral and Organizational Barriers to Faculty and Staff
Alvin Evans and Edna Breinig Chun
ASHE Higher Education Report: Volume 33, Number 1
Kelly Ward, Lisa E. Wolf-Wendel, Series Editors

ISSN 1551-6970   electronic ISSN 1554-6306   ISBN 978-04701-76849

The ASHE Higher Education Report is part of the Jossey-Bass Higher and Adult Education Series and is published six times a year by Wiley Subscription Services, Inc., A Wiley Company, at Jossey-Bass, 989 Market Street, San Francisco, California 94103-1741.

For subscription information, see the Back Issue/Subscription Order Form in the back of this volume.

CALL FOR PROPOSALS: Prospective authors are strongly encouraged to contact Kelly Ward (kaward@wsu.edu) or Lisa Wolf-Wendel (lwolf@ku.edu). See "About the ASHE Higher Education Report Series" in the back of this volume.

Visit the Jossey-Bass Web site at **www.josseybass.com.**

Contents

Executive Summary

In 1903, sociologist W.E.B. DuBois wrote that higher education is obligated to transcend the practical—by preparing students for future careers—and promote "that fine adjustment between real life and the growing knowledge of life." Transferring this insight to the workplace in higher education today finds that clear challenges remain for higher education leadership in creating an inclusive and welcoming environment for diverse faculty and staff. Faced with the need to deliver high-quality education and conduct leading-edge research in an increasingly competitive global economy, universities must foster and sustain workplace environments that ensure the retention of diverse talent. Further, as student populations become increasingly diverse, institutions of higher education must provide an education that prepares students for civic engagement and promotes the values of diversity and inclusion through curricular offerings, programs, and institutional practices. Diversity and quality are linked in terms of the achievement of institutional success, excellence, and distinction.

In response to these needs, this monograph focuses on emerging literature describing contemporary behavioral and organizational barriers facing minority and women tenure-track faculty and senior-level administrators at public research universities. It presents a cross-disciplinary approach that draws on research from the social and life sciences and social justice education to address several questions: What are the principal behavioral and organizational barriers to a diverse faculty and staff? What vocabulary can be used to describe these barriers? What are the demonstrated psychological and health-related impacts of these barriers on women and minority faculty and administrators?

How do the barriers affect the efforts of universities to achieve structural representation through hiring, tenure, retention, and promotion? What are the stages of diversity development on campuses? What proactive strategies and approaches can universities use to surmount behavioral and organizational obstacles and create a culture of inclusion?

In the course of the discussion, the monograph examines the paradox of affirmative action efforts, which have had only modest impact over the past fifty years on the hiring and retention of minority faculty and staff. Arguing that barriers to diversity in the twenty-first century have become more subtle and difficult to detect, the monograph explores typical forms of behavioral repression and discusses the effects of forms of psychological oppression on self-concept and self-esteem for both targets and agents. In this context, the book discusses the psychology of the agents of oppression who knowingly or unknowingly may perpetuate stereotypes and accept and internalize the legacy of privilege. By identifying and decoding the new "second-generation" forms of everyday discrimination, women and minority faculty and staff can protect self-esteem and develop successful ways of surmounting hidden discriminatory barriers.

The major focus of the monograph is to identify and increase understanding of the organizational and behavioral barriers to diversity that still remain in the university workplace. In this context, the monograph introduces the model of reciprocal empowerment as a framework for creating an inclusive and welcoming culture (Prilleltensky and Gonick, 1994). Reciprocal empowerment is founded on the precepts of self-determination (defining one's own identity without the fear of discrimination), distributive justice (providing equitable access to resources), and collaboration (participation in decision making) (Prilleltensky and Gonick, 1994). The model provided by reciprocal empowerment illuminates how twenty-first-century institutional diversity programs can be developed, evaluated, and sustained.

As university leaders implement a comprehensive, unified diversity strategy, the natural tendency of diversity programming to reside in pockets of the institution will be transformed. In creating a cohesive diversity strategic plan, the book includes tools for diagnosing the current state of diversity and examples from best practices in public research university environments throughout the United States. The primary goal of the monograph is to assist educational leaders, policymakers, governing boards, department chairs, and administrators in removing barriers to diversity and in making the needed adjustments that will promote the inclusion, participation, and retention of women and minority faculty and staff in the higher education workplace.

Foreword

This monograph by Alvin Evans and Edna Breinig Chun is one of three recent works published in this series that address diversity in higher education. Each monograph offers a distinct perspective on diversity while confirming that responding to diversity is necessary for institutional vitality. To understand the contribution made by this monograph, it is helpful to review the content of the other two monographs. The first volume, Daryl Smith's *The Challenge of Diversity* (originally published in 1989 and reissued in 2005), establishes that institutions of higher education continue to lag when it comes to providing access to historically underrepresented students, faculty, and administrators; creating a supportive campus climate; diversifying the curriculum; and transforming themselves to be truly diverse. Smith establishes a framework for thinking about diversity issues, suggesting that diversity is an opportunity rather than a problem. Her monograph is clear that the viability of institutions of higher education is contingent on their positive response to the challenge of diversity.

The second monograph in the series, Adalberto Aguirre Jr. and Ruben Martinez's *Diversity Leadership in Higher Education* (2007), builds on Smith's monograph by focusing on the leadership component of higher education in response to diversity. It is aimed at getting institutional leaders to move beyond co-optation strategies of diversity toward transformational approaches. Aguirre and Martinez provide thought-provoking ideas about how institutional leaders and scholars can approach diversity and bring about substantive change to higher education.

Unlike the first two monographs, which are broad in scope, this monograph by Evans and Chun is more narrowly focused. *Are the Walls Really Down?* relies on interdisciplinary lenses to explore the campus climate for diversity for faculty and administrators in the context of research universities. The interdisciplinary nature of the monograph is one of its strengths. Most noteworthy and novel is the authors' use of a biopsychosocial framework that outlines the physical impact of discrimination on those who experience oppression. This model makes the link between oppression in the workplace and physical vulnerability to illness and other health-related outcomes.

Another important contribution of this monograph is the description and use of the model of reciprocal empowerment to address diversity concerns. Reciprocal empowerment suggests that changing the institutional climate should happen through collaboration between faculty and institutional leaders. Chun and Evans go beyond offering a merely theoretical discussion of diversity: they use their experiences as practitioners in the field to provide clear examples, strategies, policies, and programs that institutions of higher education can use to improve the campus climate. The monograph offers a tool kit for changing higher education by providing concrete advice for institutions to be more receptive and responsive to diversity.

This monograph will appeal to multiple audiences. Those on campus concerned with or stymied by diversity issues are sure to find it useful. The monograph can help facilitate conversations among faculty members, administrators, and department chairs. Scholars of higher education will find this monograph offers perspectives that deserve continued exploration and analysis. Evans and Chun's monograph can play an important role in helping campus stakeholders move forward in their efforts to create more supportive campus climates for faculty and administrators. The monograph is an especially meaningful contribution, as issues associated with diversity continue to be critical to the theory and practice of higher education.

Lisa E. Wolf-Wendel
Series Editor

Acknowledgments

This monograph is dedicated to the memory of two great pioneers who contributed to the mentoring and professional success of women and minorities in higher education and the field of medicine. The late Dr. Esther Briney Chu (1911–2002), mother of Edna Breinig Chun, crossed the bridges between the cultures of America and China and, as a professor of American history at Hunter College and Jersey City State College, lobbied for women faculty members' rights in higher education when those issues had only begun to gain national attention. The late Dr. Barbara Evans (1955–2006), wife of Alvin Evans, led the way for minority women in the field of medicine and shared her success and expertise tirelessly through her work in Ghana until her untimely passing.

We wish to particularly acknowledge the contributions of Professor Maria Lima and Professor Elaine Cleeton at the State University of New York at Geneseo for their insights and inspiration throughout the process of preparing the manuscript. We also wish to thank Willis Walker, chief legal counsel at Kent State University, and Professor Ulrich Pongs for their continuous support and contributions. We especially thank our reviewers, Dr. Rohini Anand, senior vice president and chief diversity officer at Sodexho, Professor Cathy DuBois of Kent State University, Dr. Lev Gonick, vice president for information systems at Case Western Reserve University, Dr. Steve Michaels, vice provost for academic initiatives and diversity at Kent State University, Lawrence Nichols, vice president for human resources at Clemson University, and Professor Winston Thompson, associate dean of social sciences at Broward Community College, for their generous support despite very demanding schedules. We thank the anonymous reviewers for their valuable suggestions, Bryan Cook, senior research associate at the American Council on Education, and Sean Simone for their help in obtaining the most current statistical data. We acknowledge the able and thorough research assistance of Kimberly Thompson and Jessica Allen. Finally, we gratefully acknowledge the guidance of our editor, Professor Lisa Wolf-Wendel, throughout the course of preparing the monograph.

 Published online in Wiley InterScience
(www.interscience.wiley.com) • DOI: 10.1002/aehe.3301

The Theoretical Framework: Psychosocial Oppression and Diversity

The function of the university is not simply to teach breadwinning, or to furnish teachers for the public schools or to be a centre of polite society; it is, above all, to be the organ of that fine adjustment *between real life and the growing knowledge of life, an adjustment which forms the secret of civilization.*

—W.E.B. DuBois
The Souls of Black Folk, 2005 [1903], p. 85

MORE THAN A CENTURY AGO, the Harvard-trained sociologist W.E.B. DuBois identified the vision of the university as the nexus or interconnection between real life and the knowledge of life. He saw the fine adjustment between reality and the growing knowledge of reality as the secret of our civilization. This insight relates to the twenty-first-century challenge of the university to educate and prepare students for futures in a pluralistic and diverse world. Colleges and universities bear special responsibilities not only as custodians of knowledge that create, disseminate, and perpetuate knowledge in society but also as institutions with "*moral* responsibilities to maintain the well-being of society" (Wilcox and Ebbs, 1992, p. xix).

Yet ironically in the university itself, women and minorities who serve as faculty and administrators still encounter hidden barriers that obstruct their empowerment, participation, and retention. The delicate adjustment that DuBois described as the purpose of the university can be applied to the goal of achieving genuine inclusion in the walls of higher education itself.

This monograph focuses on the subtle behavioral and organizational barriers that hinder the recruitment, retention, and advancement of women and minority faculty and administrators in higher education today. Specifically the monograph explores the obstacles that face women and minorities who serve as full-time, tenure-track faculty and senior-level administrators in the context of public, doctoral-granting research universities. Discussion of behavioral and organizational barriers leads later in the monograph to identification of best practices for improvement.

The focus on racial and ethnic minorities and women in this monograph derives from the fact that the fundamental challenges related to the hiring and inclusion of minorities and women in higher education have not yet been met. Only limited progress has been made in the hiring of racial and ethnic minorities as faculty and administrators over the past quarter century, with somewhat better progress achieved in the hiring of nonminority women (Rai and Critzer, 2000). In this context, the monograph examines the success of affirmative action and explores the interrelationship between diversity and affirmative action.

The selection of public research universities for the study is based on several factors. Perhaps because of their size, resources, and legal reporting requirements, public research universities have been in the forefront in the development of institutional diversity plans. Almost all research universities must file annual affirmative action plans, as they are recipients of $50,000 or more in federal contracts. Certain commonalities exist among public research institutions in terms of greater reliance on a workforce of full-time tenure-track or tenured faculty with terminal degrees, some level of state funding support, and accountability to public constituencies. Public research universities employ approximately 18 percent of the total faculty workforce, with 128,239 faculty in the ranks of assistant, associate, and full professor (Trower and Chait, 2002; U.S. Department of Education, 2003b).

Moreover, data compiled in 2001 by the Higher Education Research Institute at the University of California at Los Angeles reveal that whereas women make up 48 percent of the professoriat at two-year colleges and 38 percent at baccalaureate-granting institutions, they make up only 28 percent of the workforce at research universities (Wilson, 2004). Slower movement toward tenure for women, lower rates of pay, and less representation in the workforce indicate that advancement for women in academe appears most difficult in research universities (Wilson, 2004).

Research universities also tend to share common institutional values such as an emphasis on research as the paramount role of faculty and the centrality of the faculty role in shaping curriculum (Toma, Dubrow, and Hartley, 2005). Research universities focus not only on the transmission of knowledge but also on its creation. The relatively homogeneous structure of the faculty career progression at these institutions makes them in effect "strategic research sites" that provide an opportunity to examine progress in attaining racial and gender equity among highly educated workers (Kulis, Chong, and Shaw, 1999, p. 117).

Overview of the Framework

The discussion begins with a brief review of the importance of reaffirming the need for diversity in higher education. What is the "business case" for diversity and inclusion in higher education today? Following this preparatory exploration, we introduce three dimensions in the framework for understanding contemporary forms of workplace discrimination. First, we seek to develop an appropriate terminology to identify and elucidate how forms of prejudice and discrimination remain embedded in institutions of higher education in the United States (Feagin and O'Brien, 2003). From this perspective, discrimination is seen not from an individualistic perspective but as a systemic social phenomenon that is socially generated and lodged in institutions whether consciously or unconsciously (Feagin and O'Brien, 2003). The terminology used to conceptualize how discrimination occurs in the workplace derives from social justice philosophy and the social sciences.

As a second dimension of the discussion, we introduce a metaphorical perspective by identifying silence as an indicator of when minorities and women are ignored and marginalized. The metaphorical perspective for describing how discrimination occurs captures the qualitative nature of how subtle behavioral forms of workplace discrimination are experienced. A third critical dimension of our exploration draws on emerging research documenting the physiological impact of discrimination on minorities and women.

After introduction of these three dimensions that illuminate contemporary workplace discrimination, the discussion culminates in the exposition of the theme of reciprocal empowerment (Prilleltensky and Gonick, 1994). Reciprocal empowerment embodies the manner in which mutual respect, recognition of individual identity and distinctiveness, the sharing of power, and the realization of each individual's potential can be realized in the higher education workplace.

The Importance of Reaffirming Diversity in Higher Education

For higher education leadership, diversity is not a choice: it is a practical imperative. With the changing demographics of student populations and the emergence by 2060 of a "minority majority" country, faculty and staff on university and college campuses must reflect the increasingly diverse nature of the United States population; homogeneity is not an alternative. A number of important arguments underscore the need for the hiring and retention of diverse and talented faculty and administrators.

Engagement

As a rationale for pursuing diversity, the concept of engagement is an emerging framework that elevates the role of faculty service by acknowledging the role of engagement in contexts that extend beyond the campus (Ward, 2003). This expanded view of scholarship understands the two-way relationship involved in the transmission of knowledge based on the synergy achieved through knowledge flowing in from the wider community to the campus as well as knowledge flowing out from the campus to the community (Ward, 2003). As a result, the engaged campus "builds on higher education's contribution to society and to a history of higher education that has always been inextricably intertwined with the larger purposes of American society" (Ward, 2003. p. 14).

The engaged campus is by necessity a diverse campus, because it prepares students for roles, careers, and leadership in a world that has been newly defined as "flat" (Friedman, 2005). The "flatness" of today's world refers to the fact that the world is a single global network in which all knowledge centers are connected and individuals collaborate and compete globally (Friedman, 2005). In this new universe, convergence is the norm rather than the exception, and value is created horizontally through multiple forms of collaboration (Friedman, 2005).

Talent Management

The compelling need for diversity among faculty and administrators in higher education is also based on the demand for talent to build and sustain institutional excellence in a global context. Talent is the engine that drives creative scholarship, fuels research and service initiatives, supports community, and ignites the educational process. Talent is an essential and differentiating factor in furthering the goals of the academy. Talented faculty bring innovation, disciplinary expertise, new research perspectives, and successful pedagogical approaches to the table. Talented administrators enhance institutional capabilities through innovation, speed, efficiency, technological know-how, and social capabilities such as leadership, collaboration, communication, and a shared mind-set (Ulrich and Smallwood, 2004). From this perspective, the ability to recruit and retain talented and diverse faculty and staff is the single most important source of strategic competitive advantage for colleges and universities today. To attain competitive advantage, public research universities must not only create proactive personnel policies and approaches but also simultaneously address the need for retention of diverse and talented faculty and administrators.

In this regard, the phenomenon of the revolving door among underrepresented faculty is documented in a study of twenty-eight institutions in California during 2000 to 2004 (Moreno and others, 2006). Specifically, 58 percent of all new underrepresented minority hires were simply replacing similar faculty who had left the institution. Despite considerable hiring efforts, the net increase of underrepresented minority faculty was only 2 percent (Moreno and others, 2006). These statistics reveal that unless hiring efforts are counterbalanced by strong retention efforts, only minimal gains in the numbers of underrepresented hires will be achieved and replenishment of the reservoir of talent will require repetitive, costly, and time-consuming efforts.

Civic Preparation

From the perspective of students' success, graduates of campuses that empower diverse faculty and administrators are better prepared not only in terms of knowledge but also with the mind-set and values needed to meet the challenges of a global society. Evidence of the impact of diversity in promoting student learning outcomes (critical thinking, intellectual engagement) and democracy outcomes (citizenship, engagement, racial and cultural understanding) has been demonstrated in a study that links data from the University of Michigan with national data (Gurin, Dey, Hurtado, and Gurin, 2002). Another study indicates that diversity enriches the educational outcomes of undergraduates and that the "vitality, stimulation, and educational potential of an institution are directly related to the composition of the student body, faculty, and staff" (Milem, Chang, and Antonio, 2005, p. 16). And from a psychological perspective, creation of a social and intellectual atmosphere different from what is familiar enhances the cognitive and identity development of students (Milem, Chang, and Antonio, 2005). Ultimately, however, students' perceptions of the level of commitment of the campus to diversity determine whether or not they can directly benefit from the diversity present in the environment (Milem, Chang, and Antonio, 2005).

Institutional Quality

The psychosocial environment and administrative practices of a campus are key institutional characteristics that influence institutional quality, engagement, and success (Smith and Wolf-Wendel, 2005). In 2005, the Association of American Colleges and Universities launched an initiative called "inclusive excellence" that links diversity and quality. Diversity and quality combine to form an alloy that is different from its constituent elements—both stronger and more durable (Clayton-Pedersen and Musil, 2005). Because institutional distinctiveness derives from an organizational culture that embodies commitment to a common theme or values translated into concrete programs and practices (Townsend, Newell, and Wiese, 1992), diversity and quality provide an opportunity for institutional differentiation. With the support of effective leadership, diversity can *transform* institutional culture and pedagogical approaches (Aguirre and Martinez, 2002) and create a legacy of institutional distinctiveness.

Accreditation

Certainly one of the most critical external drivers for achieving diversity over the past two decades is the accreditation process. Accrediting agencies have increasingly emphasized the importance of diversity, demanding evidence of concrete and tangible actions related to the incorporation of diversity in campus programs and practices. Accreditation processes have helped foster increased awareness of the importance of a cohesive and systemic approach to diversity in relation to institutional mission, strategic goals, programs, and practices.

What are the critical factors in reaffirming the need for diversity in public research universities today? The research university of the twenty-first century has become "self-consciously global" and plays a powerful role in global integration and stability as well as international mutual understanding (Levin, 2006). As a global force, the university needs to draw on the talents of a diverse workforce to build and sustain institutional excellence and foster research programs that advance knowledge. Talented and diverse faculty and administrators enhance institutional capability through leading-edge research, creative accomplishments, innovative approaches to teaching and learning, and scholarship that reflects a rich plurality of perspectives.

For the engaged campus, the transmission of knowledge represents the convergence of knowledge that flows from the campus to the wider community and back. As the student population reflects demographic population changes, the university in turn seeks to provide an education that exceeds the campus boundaries—it produces students who are "global thinkers and actors" (Lima, 2003). When incorporated into pedagogical approaches, diversity changes social mind-sets, nurtures multicultural life experiences, and challenges traditional power arrangements (Aguirre and Martinez, 2002). The public research university must not only maintain accountability to state and federal mandates but also respond systematically to accreditation reviews.

Reaffirming the need for diversity in higher education is an acknowledgment of the unique role played by the university as a social force that leverages the talents of faculty and administrators to fulfill its educational purposes. From this perspective, diversity is a connector—connecting the knowledge attained within the walls of higher education to the reality of life.

Structural Change Through Affirmative Action: A Report Card

Has progress been made in the past half century in remedying underrepresentation in higher education employment as a direct result of affirmative action? Affirmative action is a federally mandated program that addresses the hiring and advancement of racial and ethnic minorities, women, persons with disabilities, and Vietnam veterans; it differs explicitly from diversity, a word that encompasses a broad range of demographic, cultural, and personal differences.

In fact, only small gains in minority hiring have been made; apparently white women received the greatest benefit from affirmative action in both faculty and administrative ranks (Rai and Critzer, 2000). Of all the groups studied, white women were the most successful in obtaining faculty and administrative positions. Even the changes achieved by women, however, can be described as "glacial" and "excruciatingly slow" (Marschke, Laursen, Nielsen, and Rankin, 2007, p. 1). The following sections analyze overall progress from the perspective of faculty and administrators in both public and private colleges and universities, specifically compared with public research universities. For the purposes of this analysis, the definition of "administrators" is derived from the Fair Labor Standards Act: persons whose assignments involve management of an institution or a department or subdivision and who perform work related to policies or general business operations requiring discretion and judgment (U.S. Department of Education, 2003a).

Administrative Progress

In administrative ranks, white women realized the largest gains, increasing their share in these positions from one-fourth to one-third between 1979 and 1991 (Rai and Critzer, 2000). Similarly, between 1993 and 2003, the percentage of white women in administration rose from 35.1 percent to 40.7 percent, with the percentage of minority women increasing from 6.7 percent to 9.6 percent in the same time period (Harvey and Anderson, 2005; Rai and Critzer, 2000; U.S. Department of Education, 2003a).

From the perspective of minority representation in the administrative ranks, the number of positions held by African American employees rose from

4.3 percent in 1983 to 9.7 percent in 2003 (Rai and Critzer, 2000; U.S. Department of Education, 2003a). African American females made most of these gains, while the black male employment rate remained virtually unchanged, a trend that continued over this time period (U.S. Department of Education, 2003a). African American representation as administrators in public research universities, however, was only 7.6 percent (U.S. Department of Education, 2003a). The representation of Asian American females in administration actually declined in this time period but rose to 1.4 percent in 2003 (Harvey and Anderson, 2005; U.S. Department of Education, 2003a). Although severely underrepresented in 1979 (0.13 percent), representation of Hispanic women in postsecondary education administration more than doubled as of 2003 (2.2 percent) (U.S. Department of Education, 2003a), suggesting that representation of Hispanic women will eventually surpass that of Asian women in higher education administration. This greater representation reflects the fact that the Latino/Hispanic population is the fastest-growing population in the United States (Haub, 2006).

Faculty Gains

Of full-time faculty between 1983 and 1991, white women's participation rose from 24.8 percent in 1983 to 28.5 percent in 1991 and by 2003 had reached 31.9 percent (Rai and Critzer, 2000; U.S. Department of Education, 2003b). Minority women by 2003 represented only 6.5 percent of the full-time faculty workforce (U.S. Department of Education, 2003b).

During the same time period, the representation of African American faculty remained relatively low, making up 5 percent or less of the total faculty in 1991 (Rai and Critzer, 2000). This level of representation continued virtually unchanged between 1993 and 2003, with the percentage of African American faculty in 2003 still hovering at only 5.3 percent (U.S. Department of Education, 2003b). The number of African American faculty holding tenure-track positions in predominantly white institutions of higher learning, in fact, actually declined for an extended period beginning in the mid-1970s (Smith and Witt, 1996). Despite the fact that black women attained full professor rank at a rate higher than black men, black men still retained more than twice as many full professor positions in 1991 compared with black women (2,466 versus 1,106) (Zapata, 1995). Asian Americans made progress among the faculty, with females hired more frequently than males. Representation of Hispanic faculty increased rather slowly, and only 2.1 percent of full professors were Hispanic in 1991, rising to 3.2 percent in 2003, with women again surpassing men in the rate of progress (Rai and Critzer, 2000; U.S. Department of Education, 2003b).

Public research universities have been relatively less successful in hiring full-time African American and Hispanic faculty than all institutions combined, although they have a higher representation of Asian American faculty compared with all colleges and universities (U.S. Department of Education, 2003b). A review of data from 1989 reveals the same trend that has persisted over two decades: Asian American faculty have their highest level of representation in public universities and African American faculty their lowest (Milem and Astin, 1993).

Specifically, in public research universities, full-time African American faculty hold only 3.6 percent of ladder-rank positions (assistant, associate, and full professor) and 3.4 percent of ranked and unranked full-time positions. By contrast, in all institutions, African American faculty hold 5.3 percent of all full-time faculty positions. Hispanics hold only 2.7 percent of ladder-rank positions and 2.2 percent of ranked and unranked positions in public research universities (versus 3.2 percent in all institutions). Asian Americans hold 8.3 percent of positions with faculty rank in public research universities and 7.8 percent of both ranked and unranked full-time positions, whereas in all institutions they hold 6.6 percent of full-time faculty positions (U.S. Department of Education, 2003b). The patterns for employment of Asian American faculty reflect the greater concentration of these faculty in the natural sciences, mathematics, and engineering (Finkelstein, Seal, and Schuster, 1998).

Once having gained entry to the workplace, women continue to face significant challenges in attaining tenure and reaching the highest faculty ranks. Based on 1999 National Study of Postsecondary Faculty data, the odds of holding a nontenured position are approximately 1.5 times greater for women (Perna, 2005). Only 18 percent of women, compared with 38 percent of male full-time faculty, hold tenured positions, and the gap does not appear to be closing (Perna, 2005). This finding occurs even after controlling for measures

TABLE 1

2003 Race and Gender of Administrative, Executive, and Managerial Staff at Public Doctoral Research Universities

American Indian			Asian/Pacific Islander			Black			Hispanic			White			Nonresident			Unknown		
M	F	Both	M	F	Both	M	F	Both	M	F	Both	M	F	Both	M	F	Both	M	F	Both
0.3%	0.3%	0.5%	1.4%	1.3%	2.7%	3.3%	4.3%	7.6%	1.7%	1.8%	3.5%	46.2%	37.8%	83.9%	0.3%	0.1%	0.5%	0.6%	0.8%	1.4%

Source: U.S. Department of Education, 2003a.

TABLE 2

2003 Race and Gender of Full-Time Faculty at Public Doctoral Research Universities with Tenure Systems (Percent Within Rank)

	American Indian			Asian/Pacific Islander			Black			Hispanic			White			Nonresident			Unknown		
	M	F	Both	M	F	Both	M	F	Both	M	F	Both	M	F	Both	M	F	Both	M	F	Both
Full Professor	0.2%	0.1%	0.3%	6.7%	0.9%	7.6%	1.5%	0.7%	2.2%	1.6%	0.4%	2.0%	71.4%	15.8%	87.2%	0.5%	0.0%	0.5%	0.2%	0.1%	0.3%
Associate Professor	0.3%	0.2%	0.5%	6.1%	1.9%	8.0%	2.6%	2.1%	4.7%	1.9%	1.2%	3.1%	53.5%	28.6%	82.1%	0.9%	0.3%	1.2%	0.3%	0.1%	0.4%
Assistant Professor	0.3%	0.3%	0.5%	6.6%	3.5%	10.1%	2.2%	2.8%	5.0%	2.0%	1.7%	3.8%	39.6%	29.2%	68.8%	7.4%	2.9%	10.3%	0.9%	0.6%	1.5%
Total	0.2%	0.2%	0.4%	6.5%	1.8%	8.3%	2.0%	1.6%	3.6%	1.8%	1.0%	2.7%	58.2%	22.9%	81.1%	2.3%	0.8%	3.2%	0.4%	0.2%	0.6%

Source: U.S. Department of Education, 2003b.

of productivity, structural characteristics (type of institution, discipline), human capital (educational attainment, experience, and mobility) and family ties. The concentration of women in lower ranks of the academic ladder cannot be explained fully by other variables (Perna, 2005).

As a result, women faculty tend to reside in lower-rank positions with less power. Women and minorities are more heavily represented in non-tenure-track positions than full-time positions, limiting their progress up the academic career ladder (Dugger, 2001). Differential outcomes in hiring, reappointment, tenure, and promotion as well as salary discrepancies between men and women faculty persist (Cooper and Stevens, 2002b; Granger, 1993; Gregory, 2001; Johnsrud and Des Jarlais, 1994; Kulis, 1997; Marschke, Laursen, Nielsen, and Rankin, 2007; Park, 1996; Winkler, 2000). Despite modest increases in the aggregate number of women faculty, the types and levels of positions women and minorities hold in higher education and their opportunities for advancement must be taken into consideration in assessing the success of affirmative action.

Why Is a Cross-Disciplinary Framework for Achieving Diversity Needed?

Despite the challenges posed by differing organizational structures and cultures in higher education, a dynamic conceptual framework is needed to capture the fundamental dilemma underlying the struggles of minority and women faculty and to propose a process for improvement. The model will benefit from a cross-disciplinary perspective drawn from the life and social sciences and social justice education to provide a holistic framework for understanding and overcoming barriers to diversity. As Wilson (1998) points out, a cross-disciplinary framework provides a way of explaining and understanding complex problems through *consilience*. The word "consilience" means literally a "jumping together" of knowledge by the linking of facts and fact-based theory across disciplines to create a common groundwork of explanation (Wilson, 1998).

Whereas the natural sciences have long understood the importance of surmounting disciplinary boundaries in solving complex problems, the social sciences and humanities have not similarly joined with the natural sciences in the search for unified understanding. Consilience offers a new vista in understanding the human condition, as most real-world problems exist in a realm without maps, with few concepts and words, and where the disciplines intersect (Wilson, 1998). Solutions require fluency across the boundaries to "provide a clear view of the world as it really is" (Wilson, 1998, p. 13). By applying a dynamic conceptual framework to our investigation of barriers to achieving faculty and staff diversity in higher education, the complexity of these barriers can be understood from multiple perspectives. Recognition of existing barriers will lead to the development and synthesis of comprehensive strategies for making the fine adjustments needed to achieve faculty and staff diversity.

Asymmetric Institutional Power and Oppression

This monograph will examine how power is transmitted in the higher education workplace and its subsequent impact on minority and women faculty and staff. It will explore how subtle forms of discrimination remain in the higher education environment, whether consciously or unconsciously, through the collective impact of organizational and behavioral barriers to diversity. Practical strategies for overcoming these barriers will require surmounting both structural and behavioral obstacles.

To understand the nature of psychosocial oppression, the monograph draws on theoretical perspectives developed by researchers in the social sciences and social justice education over the past decade (Bell, 1997; Collins, 1993; Goodman, 2001; Hardiman and Jackson, 1997; Kincheloe and Steinberg, 1998; Prilleltensky and Gonick, 1994; Razack, 1998). Their findings remain relevant and even controversial today. Through these scholars' bold exploration of the roots of the "isms"—racism, sexism, ableism—the pervasive residue of *oppression,* which still threads its way through the context of institutional life, whether in classrooms or boardrooms, is exposed.

But first, to view oppression, we must change the focus that normally governs our socially derived ways of seeing and recognize that historical legacies of oppression have structured our understandings of each other and that our actions often reproduce these social hierarchies (Razack, 1998). The concept of "positionality," which governs the way we understand the world and others, and in particular the concept of white positionality will enable us to unravel the complex threads of power relations that have evolved into systems of inequality (Kincheloe and Steinberg, 1998). From this theoretical perspective, whiteness is a "social construction in that it can be invented, lived, analyzed, modified and discarded" (Kincheloe and Steinberg, 1998, p. 8). In this sense, whiteness is affected by cultural, political, economic, and social contexts (Kincheloe and Steinberg, 1998).

Power, resistance, and domination are the ways that oppression is manifested in the suppression of human diversity (Prilleltensky and Gonick, 1994). Theories of systemic, institutional discrimination identify both direct and indirect ways that dominant groups seek to maintain privileged status in the workplace (Kulis, 1997). Oppression involves asymmetric power relations where dominating groups limit access to material resources and infuse in marginalized groups self-deprecating perceptions of themselves (Prilleltensky and Gonick, 1994). Privilege can be contained in organizational norms, recruitment procedures, informal networks, decision-making processes, and job allocation procedures (Kulis, 1997).

Oppression has two primary dimensions: the internal psychosocial view relating to the individual's capability and the external structured view that is part of the political-economic context (Prilleltensky and Gonick, 1994). The psychosocial and structured viewpoints provide the keys to understanding the impact and dual nature of behavioral (internal) and organizational (external) barriers to diversity in higher education.

Contemporary forms of oppression need not involve forms of political or economic inequality but can exist exclusively in the form of psychic alienation or internalized oppression in which those who have been psychologically oppressed become their own oppressors (Bartky, 1990, cited in Prilleltensky and Gonick, 1994). The collusion of members of oppressed groups in their own oppression reflects the internalization of oppression. "Collusion" refers to the fact that individuals from marginalized groups may think, act, and feel in a manner that reflects the devaluation of their group (Hardiman and Jackson, 1997). The concept of hegemony explains how power is sustained not only through coercion but also through the voluntary consent of the targets. The view of a dominant group can be projected so successfully that it "is accepted as common sense, as part of the natural order, even by those who are in fact disempowered by it" (Bell, 1997, p. 11).

For example, a woman faculty member undergoing difficult tenure processes may develop a deep sense of shame and believe that she deserves to be treated badly ("Tenure in a Chilly Climate," 1999). She may think, "If only I had published more, gotten better teaching reviews, voted differently, had more colleagues over for dinner, not worn jeans, used more makeup ..." (p. 91).

Another personal account of resisting internalization of oppression is provided by a minority woman scholar named Inez in an interview in a large public research university: "One of the things that concerns me greatly is the number of women of color who leave here believing that it was something they did, or the number of women of color who stay here under that same misconception. I think we need to tell our horror stories to one another so we're not afraid that it really is our problem" (Thomas and Hollenshead, 2001, p. 71).

From a general perspective, oppression is pervasive and institutional, restricts life opportunities, involves hierarchical relationships, and may invoke multiple dimensions linked together in an "overarching system of domination" (Bell, 1997, p. 5). Hardiman and Jackson's social oppression model (1997) examines the impact of oppression at three levels: individual, institutional, and cultural/societal. Oppression shapes social and institutional reality in four major ways that can be understood in a linear perspective. First, the group in power defines and controls reality, including what is viewed as normal or correct. Second, whether conscious or unconscious, acts of marginalization and discrimination become institutionalized and systematized. Third, psychological colonization occurs when the target group internalizes the oppression and colludes with the dominant group's values and social system. Fourth, the dominant group's culture is imposed while the target group's history and culture are discounted (Hardiman and Jackson, 1997).

The interlocking nature of race, gender, and class oppression recurs as a theme in research over the past three decades (Collins, 1993; Razack, 1998). The viewpoint of oppression that uncovers the intersection of multiple structures of domination provides a "clearer view of oppression" than that of "other groups who occupy more contradictory positions vis-à-vis white male power," as minority women cannot use whiteness to negate female subordination or use maleness to neutralize the stigma of being black (Collins, 1993, p. 50). Women who are also minorities and poor experience the *simultaneity* of multiple layers of oppression (Collins, 1993). In the context of the campus environment, white males still remain the dominant power group on campus in terms of status, power, and influence, while conditions for racial and ethnic minorities tend to be worse than those for white women (Ponterotto, 1990a).

The simultaneity of the interlocking systems of oppression is most apparent in the sheer "physicality of the encounter between powerful and powerless groups and the importance of the visible in colonial encounters—who and what is seen and not seen" (Razack, 1998, p. 15). Both the cultural differences approach and the rights approach to education fail to consider the historical legacies of oppression that structure groups unequally (Razack, 1998). The cultural differences approach focuses on the cultural characteristics of minority groups as if their lifestyle and culture were the obstacles to communication across differences. It simplistically assumes that individuals with the correct information and some practice can stand innocently outside hierarchical social relations and view marginalized groups as having certain characteristics that can be studied and managed (Razack, 1998). Similarly, the rights approach assumes that all parties have had and continue to have equal rights in the social context while viewing oppressed groups simply as different and less developed (Razack, 1998).

The Antidote for Oppression: Reciprocal Empowerment

Given the existence of psychosocial oppression, what force can be applied in the context of higher education to counterbalance and overcome its strength? The antidote for oppression lies in *reciprocal empowerment* (Prilleltensky and Gonick, 1994). Although the word "empowerment" has frequently been mentioned in human resource and management theory, the potential reciprocity of empowerment has not been recognized. The unidirectional concept of empowerment without reciprocity does not capture the mutual engagement needed to build and sustain respect for diversity. The concept of *ambiguous empowerment* is the antithesis of reciprocal empowerment and refers to contradictory experiences of power and subjection by marginalized groups (Chase, 1995).

Reciprocal empowerment involves the interdependence and interrelationship of both parties. Instead of the "one-up and one-down" vertical pattern of oppression that travels from target to agent (Hardiman and Jackson, 1997), reciprocal empowerment involves the sharing of power. Empowerment levels the playing field from a hierarchical context to a democratic and participatory framework (Hardiman and Jackson, 1997). In a similar vein, Thomas (1996) identifies the notion of "facilitating empowerment" as a management model that permits discretion, allows individual effectiveness rather than simply cloning behavior, and supports success through partnership and involvement.

The reciprocity involved in empowerment is diametrically opposed to conditions that create contingency. From a historical perspective, American society both before and after the emancipation of slavery "sought to impose a state of non-being on black Americans" and to impose conditions of both contingency and precariousness (Roberts, 1999, p. 4). Contingency means depriving an individual of his or her autonomy, will, and self-governance, while precariousness imposes instability so that the individual cannot create a sense of order in his or her existence. In this historical context, the efforts of racist America to impose a state of contingency on black Americans is counterbalanced by the efforts of African Americans to seek virtue and affirm their own being (Roberts, 1999).

In contrast, reciprocity implies mutual dependence and a sense of mutual obligation: "Inherent in this situation is the self-awareness that one is called on to consider the rights and feelings of others *before* taking significant action. All human beings seek a level of reciprocity in interaction with other people. The assumption of these intricate, often unstated 'contracts' of reciprocity becomes the very foundation of the social bond" (Roberts, 1999, p. 8). Reciprocal empowerment is also a "degendered form of interaction" transcending patriarchal and even feminist models (Darlington and Mulvaney, 2003, p. 3). In this sense, reciprocal empowerment fosters an egalitarian environment that is characterized by mutual attention, mutual empathy, mutual engagement, and mutual responsiveness (Darlington and Mulvaney, 2003). Perhaps most important, as a *style* of interaction reciprocal empowerment fosters a sense of personal authority and self-confidence that can lead to action (Darlington and Mulvaney, 2003).

The concept of recognition is also closely allied with reciprocal empowerment. Recognition is a concept that bridges several disciplines, including political science and social psychology, and is at the center of American race relations (Feagin, Vera, and Imani, 1996). It implies both reciprocity and respect and captures the mutuality of reciprocal empowerment.

In the model for reciprocal empowerment provided by Prilleltensky and Gonick (1994), juxtaposed to the concepts of power, subordination, and domination are the three pillars or values of self-determination, distributive justice, and collaboration and democratic participation (see Exhibit 1). As these researchers explain, because empowerment involves the amount of control

EXHIBIT 1
Reciprocal Empowerment, Human Diversity, and Oppression: A Values-Based Approach

Values	Reciprocal Empowerment	Human Diversity	Oppression
Self-determination	The power to give to oneself and others the ability to define identity	Celebration of uniqueness and affirmation of identity despite differences	Externally produced and internalized negative view of oneself
Distributive justice	The power to give to oneself and others sufficient resources	Recognition of diversity as a resource and fair allocation of goods and burdens despite differences	Externally produced and internalized view of oneself as not deserving more resources
Collaboration and democratic participation	The power to give to oneself and others a voice in society	Equal participation in decision-making processes despite differences	Externally produced and internalized view of one's own voice as unimportant

Source: Prilleltensky and Gonick, 1994, p. 147.

individuals have over their own lives, reciprocal empowerment first refers to *self-determination* or the ability to define one's personal identity without the fear of discrimination or having identity externally imposed. Second, the concept of reciprocal empowerment involves *distributive justice* or access to resources as well as the intervention needed to ensure equitable distribution. (Affirmative action is a primary example of distributive justice.) Third, reciprocal empowerment involves *collaboration* and participation in decision making. All three components of reciprocal empowerment require intervention and struggle in that those who are already empowered must share power with marginalized groups and disempower those who refuse to share resources (Prilleltensky and Gonick, 1994). As a values-based framework grounded in moral philosophy, the attainment of personal or collective power involves the ethical imperative to share power with those in less advantageous positions (Hardiman and Jackson, 1997).

A concrete example of reciprocal empowerment in the higher education environment pertains to the remarkable success realized through a tactical strategy of the Information Technology Services Division at Case Western University in Cleveland, Ohio. A team of minority women professionals under the direction of an instructional designer have been working collaboratively with School of Medicine faculty to reinvent the medical curriculum electronically. The sharing of the team's technical and professional skills coupled with the corresponding empowerment of the faculty in redesigning the curriculum has resulted in a shift from hierarchical arrangements to a collaboration characterized by reciprocity and mutual respect (Dr. L. Gonick, personal communication, December 28, 2006).

A second example of how reciprocal empowerment has been implemented in a research university is the Sisters Mentoring Sisters project undertaken at a large, predominantly white institution with thirty-four thousand students in central Florida (Green and King, 2001). This project's purpose is to assist black women in all occupational groups at the university through an empowerment model of career advancement and leadership development (Green and King, 2001). Based on Afrocentric principles, "sister mentors" help participants overcome workplace barriers and acquire experience in formal and informal decision making in the academy (Green and King, 2001).

Another example of reciprocal empowerment as it applies to senior-level administration would benefit from the empirical research findings in corporate America relating to the career progression of minority administrators. This research, conducted over a three-year period in three major American corporations, reveals that minority executives' careers typically inched along in the early stages, whereas white professionals were frequently fast-tracked (Thomas, 2001). In a "two-tournament" system that is often "separate and unequal," mentors helped minority professionals sustain their levels of performance and prevented them from leaving the organization (Thomas, 2001, p. 101). Mentors played an important role in confronting unfair criticisms directed at their protégés by subordinates and peers, especially if the criticisms were racially motivated. Yet even when career advancement did not occur, mentoring relationships provided opportunities for professional challenges that strengthened competencies, confidence, and organizational credibility. The mentors provided inside advice about the organization and served as important sponsors who actively prevented the type of sniping that can undermine self-confidence and cause a career to derail (Thomas, 2001).

The elements of reciprocal empowerment present in this example include the role of the mentor in protecting the minority administrator from unwarranted criticism, fostering his or her self-confidence, helping him or her navigate through institutional channels, allowing the professional to develop competencies and credibility in the organization, and supporting the individual's progress. The process of empowerment in turn actualizes the leader's role as an agent of the institution who reflects its ethical values and goals.

The model of reciprocal empowerment requires higher education leaders and diversity practitioners to examine how power, resistance, and domination are manifested in administrative and decision-making processes. Because the model articulates the dual nature of oppression as both an internal and external phenomenon, it necessitates consideration of both process-oriented and psychosocial forms of oppression.

In the past, higher education leaders facing the challenge of improving diversity on their campuses have focused solely on administrative processes. In contrast, as more subtle forms of oppression have emerged in the twenty-first-century workplace, educators face greater difficulties in discerning the complex behavioral dynamics that can lead to the suppression of diversity. This dynamic may be disguised in rhetoric or contradictory messages and may reflect unconscious acceptance of the legacy of privilege.

In the context of higher education, psychological climate and behavioral dimensions influence a campus's racial and ethnic diversity (Hurtado, Milem, Clayton-Pedersen, and Allen, 1999). In determining the educational environment's receptivity for diversity, the institution's particular historical legacy of inclusion or exclusion of racial and ethnic groups as well as the extent to which structural diversity has been attained are important factors (Hurtado, Milem, Clayton-Pedersen, and Allen, 1999). Psychological climate is also a function of intergroup relationships and of how interactions among diverse groups have taken place (Hurtado, Milem, Clayton-Pedersen, and Allen, 1999; Smith and Wolf-Wendel, 2005). The concept of a "chilly climate" is a much more complex construct than first thought twenty years ago and now refers to environments that do not feel welcoming to women and minorities (Smith and Wolf-Wendel, 2005).

In this regard, the goal of reciprocal empowerment fosters the need for positive and incremental steps by higher education leaders and diversity practitioners to counteract and progressively remove the behavioral and administrative barriers that impede the full participation of women and minorities in the workplace. Reciprocal empowerment neutralizes the framework of asymmetric institutional power and provides a medium through which the campus of the future allows for the full engagement of all its members.

The Metaphorical Perspective: Silence and Disempowerment

The second perspective in the framework for understanding diversity is a metaphorical one that serves to capture the subtle and elusive nature of oppression in the higher education workplace today. The power of metaphor translates the polarities that characterize the language of social justice educators into the blended ambiguities that provide insight into the actual ways that psychosocial oppression takes place.

Although visibility and invisibility have often been suggested as the primary metaphor for the dynamics of oppression, the metaphor of sound more accurately captures the nature of oppression in subduing diversity (Reinharz, 1994). Vision or sight is relatively passive, while voice is active. Like children who were once admonished to be seen and not heard, women and minorities are both *silent* and *silenced*. In Reinharz's words, "It has never been as threatening to the powerful when powerless people are seen as when they are heard" (1994, p. 184). If women and minorities insist on being seen or heard, this insistence can result in being "smashed in the process by a wall of denial that makes of one's existence an illusion, an imagined story of unfairness and injustice" (Razack, 1998, p. 24).

Recognizing voice and silence as the dominant metaphors for power relations means that, if institutional policies support only marginalized groups as being seen or physically present without being heard, then little change has occurred (Reinharz, 1994). Historically, individuals without power were not allowed to speak. In the dynamic of power relations those with power speak while those without must ask permission or remain silent.

The silence of women and minorities in the workplace captures the dichotomy discussed earlier: the external contextual view that shapes and controls behavior and the internal psychosocial view that internalizes these realities. Silence reflects the internalization of negative attitudes and behaviors and is a sign of the individual's frustration and insecurity (Reinharz, 1994). In this regard, for example, the marginalization of minority faculty has made them silent in terms of leadership participation in higher education: "You may see them, but you can't hear them" (Aguirre and Martinez, 2002, p. 56).

As we move farther into our analysis of the higher education workplace, important questions related to the ability of women and minorities to participate by not merely being present but by providing input and engaging in decision making help gauge the level of reciprocal empowerment. Can minorities and women speak in meetings? Is their counsel sought and valued? Are their views listened to? Is their speech interrupted? Are they recognized, ignored, or overlooked?

A telling example of how women's voices are suppressed is revealed in the *Attorney's Survey Report* for the Gender Bias Committee of the Supreme

Judicial Court of Massachusetts (Reinharz, 1994). The report examines how speech is interrupted in courtroom settings and indicates that although 69 percent of female attorneys were interrupted by counsel while speaking, only 11 percent of the male attorneys were (Reinharz, 1994). The privilege to interrupt speech represents a subtle but powerful form of social control. Interrupting speech is an indicator of psychological forms of oppression and of devaluation.

In the identification of organizational and behavioral barriers, the ability to speak and to be heard are key indicators of the participation of women and minorities. When we apply the insights obtained from this metaphor, we can discern the subtle forms of power, resistance, and domination that may be hidden by the concept of merely allowing women and minorities to be present.

The metaphor of voice coupled with the dynamic of reciprocal empowerment finds parallels in the diversity paradigm developed by Thomas (1996). The acceptance of diversity is measured in a continuum of eight action options ranging from exclusion, denial, suppression, assimilation, and isolation to toleration, building relationships, and fostering mutual adaptation (Thomas, 1996). Only one of these eight action options, mutual adaptation, requires the change involved in both parties implied in reciprocal empowerment and in this sense fully embraces diversity and complexity. Like reciprocal empowerment, mutual adaptation requires that the individual uphold and reaffirm the identity of the other. Paradoxically, both sides benefit from the interaction, yet the benefits of mutuality are often overlooked.

The Biopsychosocial Framework

The impact of discrimination in creating chronic stress and heightening the risk of stress-related disease is a third important dimension in the framework for understanding diversity in the higher education workplace. This dimension of the framework identifies the hidden institutional costs of discrimination and the deleterious effects experienced by individuals who are discriminated against. The potential for significant economic cost to institutions of higher education arises through increased illness, greater use of sick leave, loss of productivity, rise in healthcare and workers' compensation claims and costs, and escalating replacement or turnover costs. Further, these psychological costs are directly tied to the elements of the campus psychosocial environment and the health of that environment.

New interdisciplinary research proposes a biopsychosocial model for understanding the differential effect of psychosocial stresses on minorities. Myers, Lewis, and Parker-Dominguez (2003) build on the work of social psychologists such as Clark, Anderson, Clark, and Williams (1999) to indicate that "at the core of ethnic health disparities is differential exposure and vulnerability to psychosocial stresses moderated by inadequate access to and control over essential material, psychological, and social resources" (Myers, Lewis, and Parker-Dominguez, 2003, p. 378). Differential vulnerability results from an imbalance in stress and resources arising from how the socially defining attributes of race, ethnicity, and social class impact life opportunities and social hierarchy (Myers, Lewis, and Parker-Dominguez, 2003). As a result, the interplay of biological, psychological, and behavioral factors can create "cumulative biobehavioral vulnerability" that is linked at least partially to persistent health disparities documented epidemiologically across generations (Myers, Lewis, and Parker-Dominguez, 2003, p. 378).

Life expectancy statistics show that black males have the shortest life expectancy of all demographic groups—69.2 years—compared with 75.4 years for white males, 80.5 years for white females, and 76.1 years for black females (Britt, 2006). In the context of such data, black men are "an endangered species" (Parham and McDavis, 1987). Black men pay a "high emotional and physical price" in the effort to survive in the workplace. They "may feel a sense of internalized anxiety, anger, frustration, and resentment because of withheld promotions, dead-end jobs, lack of policy-making power, and the necessity for them to have a 'dual identity' in hiding their reactions and feelings" (Parham and McDavis, 1987, p. 26). Feelings of depression, loss of motivation, and withdrawal can result. Stress-related diseases as well as diabetes, heart trouble, and high blood pressure are part of the physical toll that black men are likely to experience (Parham and McDavis, 1987).

Recent studies document the growing scientific evidence that identifies the profound and often prolonged physiological and mental health effects of discrimination (Jackson and Mustillo, 2001; Kessler, Mickelson, and Williams,

1999; Myers, Lewis, and Parker-Dominguez, 2003; Roberts, Swanson, and Murphy, 2004; Saez-Santiago and Bernal, 2003; Williams, Yu, Jackson, and Anderson, 1997). The adverse psychological and physiological impact of the suppression of diversity on women and minorities is an important subject for continued scientific and medical research. Coping resources that enable women and minorities to respond successfully to environmental challenges are needed to deflect and overcome the effects of workplace discrimination.

How do these physiological and mental health findings affect our understanding of oppression? Scientific research helps illuminate the potential impact of prolonged stress experienced by women and minorities through the domination of individuals who hold power in the workplace. Without sufficient outlets or mechanisms to counterbalance such stress, harmful effects can indeed lead to disease and weakening of the individual's immune system and natural bodily defense mechanisms. For example, the research of Smith and Witt (1996), based on a sample of more than one thousand faculty, reveals that African American faculty experienced greater levels of stress associated with service and research activities. The researchers attribute this increased stress to additional demands and time constraints placed on minority faculty. Further exploration of organizational and behavioral barriers in higher education will increase understanding of the potential impact such barriers have in heightening workplace stress.

The New Paradigm in Overcoming Barriers to Faculty and Staff Diversity

For far too long, higher education leadership has failed to bring real life to academe by perpetuating an institutional climate that at first excluded women and minorities and then, once they were allowed in, often frustrated their success in the higher education community. Today this leadership faces an even more urgent need to build and sustain a diverse workforce of faculty and staff while meeting the needs of an equally diverse student population in an increasingly competitive global community. From a strategic perspective, higher education leaders must look for effective ways to eliminate behavioral and organizational barriers that frustrate the ambitions of women and minority faculty and staff.

These realities of everyday life in academe are sometimes unfortunately recognized only by minorities; "white academic leaders need to learn to recognize the more common and nuanced forms of racism that persist in the academy" (Tierney and Bensimon, 1996, p. 123). As indicated earlier, the new paradigm for understanding barriers to faculty and staff diversity involves both administrative practices and the psychosocial environment. Indications of psychosocial environment can be found in the attitudes in the campus community about diversity; the level of faculty, administrative, and board support for individuals and programs; the levels of satisfaction among diverse faculty, staff and students; and the interactions among students and faculty as important components of this environment (Smith and Wolf-Wendel, 2005).

To decode the complex behaviors and internal responses that characterize the suppression of diversity, the lens must be wider and more inclusive. It must capture the subtle nature of oppression by interpreting conflicting signals and meld the insights from different disciplines into a single, cohesive picture. Further, it must unravel an often complex, unconscious behavioral dynamic and its resulting physiological impact.

Why is it important to understand these interrelationships? Academic and administrative leaders grappling with achieving diversity in the higher education workplace need to detect the symptoms and operant conditions that signal the suppression of diversity. Without appropriate cues to unveil the nature of power, resistance, and domination, the suppression of diversity can be easily masked.

This monograph examines behavioral forms of oppression as well as the physiological and mental health toll exacted by prolonged, everyday discrimination in the workplace. Only through awareness of the barriers that hamper progress and operate below the surface of organizational life can higher education leaders and administrators initiate the changes and make the adjustments necessary to achieve a "culture of diversity" (Loden and Rosener, 1991).

Affirmative Action and Diversity: Partners and Protagonists

The cruel disease of discrimination knows no sectional or state boundaries. The continuing attack on this problem must be equally broad. It must be both private and public—it must be conducted at national, state, and local levels—and it must include both legislative and executive action.

— President John F. Kennedy, February 28, 1963

BECAUSE AFFIRMATIVE ACTION HAS HAD ONLY modest success in changing the demographics of the higher education workplace, the question naturally arises as to its effectiveness and role in preparing the groundwork for reciprocal empowerment. In this regard, although affirmative action has provided an important conduit for hiring female and minority faculty and staff, its impact has been severely limited in several important respects. The data reveal that affirmative action has resulted in hiring gains for white women in higher education—but not for minorities. Despite the greater success realized in the hiring of white females, affirmative action essentially addresses only structural issues of representation that affect surface-level diversity. It has little foothold or influence on issues relating to retention, inclusion, the sharing of power, and decision making. Further, because of the backlash associated with the implementation of affirmative action, once hired minorities and women have sometimes been marginalized through the perception of tokenism (Niemann, 1999; Niemann, 2003; Turner and Myers, 2000; Yoder, Aniakudo, and Berendsen, 1996).

Although affirmative action has not proved adequate to the task of diversification and inclusion, it has been a genuine attempt to ensure that institutions of higher education are publicly accountable (Busenberg and Smith, 1997). Because of affirmative action's progress against the discrimination of women, white women now need to serve as role models in continuing their support of affirmative action to help minority colleagues (Busenberg and Smith, 1997). Because majority females have made the most significant gains in hiring over the past quarter century, they are now positioned to assist minorities to enter and navigate the higher education workplace (Busenberg and Smith, 1997). White women must still surmount the obstacles of the glass ceiling to achieve empowerment in the workplace. The alliance of women and minorities in this effort will support the achievement of the goal of reciprocal empowerment for both groups.

Even despite affirmative action's lack of success in the hiring of minorities, dismantling affirmative action would signal that institutions could turn away from the beneficial procedures and policies they have initiated under its umbrella (Busenberg and Smith, 1997). Viewed from the perspective of changing institutional demographics, affirmative action's external imperative remains critical and needed in the hiring of minorities. This chapter describes the emergence of affirmative action as a bold and specific historical strategy and contrasts it with the broader goals of diversity and inclusion. Viewing diversity as an evolving continuum, it discusses how affirmative action serves as a threshold condition for diversity, particularly in relation to underrepresented groups. Following this discussion, the concepts of culture and climate provide the context for understanding barriers and opportunities for undertaking diversity efforts in higher education.

Historical Development of Affirmative Action in Perspective

As a federal mandate, affirmative action represents an active intervention by the United States government designed to eliminate discrimination in hiring and address the underrepresentation of women and minorities in the workplaces of federal contractors. As indicated earlier, almost all public research universities today qualify as federal contractors.

Beginning with Executive Order 8802 issued by President Franklin Delano Roosevelt on June 25, 1941, which outlawed discrimination in the defense industries and government based on "race, creed, color or national origin," a clear standard of nondiscrimination was set in public employment. The order, however, did not address discrimination against women. This mandate was significantly broadened by President John F. Kennedy in 1961 with Executive Order 10925, which required that federal contractors "take affirmative action to ensure that applicants are employed, and that employees are treated during employment, without regard to their race, creed, color, or national origin." In fact, Executive Order 10925 represented a turning point in United States history by requiring not only nondiscrimination but also aggressive and positive steps by federal contractors to counteract the past effects of discrimination.

With the passage of the Civil Rights Act of 1964 and subsequent formation of the Equal Employment Opportunity Commission (EEOC), clear legal protection against overt forms of discrimination was afforded to individuals based on the protected characteristics of race, color, religion, sex, and national origin. This directive was strengthened and solidified by Executive Order 11246 issued by President Lyndon Baines Johnson in 1965, which required federal contractors to prepare annual written affirmative action plans that incorporate goals and timetables for remedying the underrepresentation of women and minorities. Because of its rigorous standards for annual compliance, affirmative action as defined in Executive Order 11246 is not simply a vague and unprescribed mandate but has specific reporting requirements with legal accountability mechanisms. The Office of Federal Contract Compliance created in 1965 within the Department of Labor monitors this compliance.

Chapter 60 of Title 41 in the Code of Federal Regulations remains the legal and statistical litmus test for assessing compliance with affirmative action standards in employment—a standard that has not been altered by recent Supreme Court decisions relating to admissions processes. Chapter 60 establishes the criteria for determining underrepresentation of minorities and women in the workforce of federal contractors and requires that affirmative action plans document "good faith" efforts on the part of employers to remedy historic underrepresentation. The specific method of determining underrepresentation is based on utilization analysis, that is, a statistical comparison between the availability of qualified women and minority workers in a given job group in the recruitment area to the actual incumbency of women and minorities in the workplace.

The intent of affirmative action has frequently been misunderstood and even mischaracterized. According to Crosby (2004), the focus of affirmative action is not on *past* but *present* wrongs. Affirmative action's development is essentially based on an ethos of distributive and procedural justice.

Distributive justice refers to the processes by which society fairly distributes its benefits such as wages, and legal rights. It is distinguished from aggregative principles in that it is concerned with how these benefits are shared among individual members of a group rather than the total good enjoyed by a given group of individuals (Prilleltensky, 1994). As a mechanism of distributive justice, affirmative action assesses the relationship between inputs and outcomes by examining structural imbalances in the availability of qualified women and minorities in a job group compared with their actual employment in an institution's workforce (Crosby, 2004). Taking it a step farther, the traditions of distributive justice underpin the development of affirmative action as a social mechanism.

Contrary to the perception that affirmative action is really a quota system, the goals established through affirmative action are statistically derived and represent a concrete target requiring good faith outreach, recruitment, and hiring efforts. Similarly, despite the claim by some critics that affirmative action requires consideration of unqualified workers, the rigorous requirement of assessing the availability of qualified women and minorities in specific job groups actually counteracts such claims.

From a philosophical standpoint, affirmative action also addresses procedural justice in terms of whether or not employment and hiring processes that appear to treat everyone equally actually do treat everyone the same way (Crosby, 2004). Seemingly neutral policies and procedures can serve to obscure how opportunities are made available and the potential for subjective disparities in the hiring process.

The Interrelationship of Affirmative Action and Diversity

Although affirmative action and diversity have distinctly different origins, scope, and foci, they function in a complementary and sequential relationship. Affirmative action is a necessary first step in the attainment of diversity, as diversity cannot be attained without the satisfactory representation of minority group members in the workplace. Whereas affirmative action seeks to affect workplace demographics based on race, gender, disability, and veteran status, diversity includes a wider array of characteristics, including generational differences, age, sexual orientation, educational background, religious beliefs, marital status, geographic location, income, and parental status (Loden and Rosener, 1991). Exhibit 2 summarizes key points of similarity and difference between affirmative action and diversity.

From a linear perspective, affirmative action opens the door to diversity by admitting minority group members. Through the hiring process, affirmative action programs provide a channel to the achievement of diversity on campus by obtaining representation for underrepresented groups. Although

EXHIBIT 2
Comparison Between Affirmative Action and Diversity

Affirmative Action	Diversity
Purposeful steps to create employment opportunities for minorities and women, disabled persons, and covered veterans	Exists in organizations with a variety of demographic, cultural, and personal differences
Narrowly focused on demographics	Broad focus
Emphasis on legal compliance. Required by law for employers with federal contracts of more than $50,000 and 50 or more employees	Voluntary programs designed to create a positive environment where no one is advantaged or disadvantaged
Addresses and prevents discrimination	Values differences
Uses statistical availability compared with representation in job groups to determine underrepresentation	Qualitative and holistic

affirmative action can enable the attainment of some measure of diversity, without affirmative action a university cannot achieve a true culture of diversity. Once affirmative action is successful in bringing underrepresented individuals into the organization, diversity programs can then work toward the achievement of retention and empowerment.

By hiring minority faculty and staff, colleges and universities lay the groundwork for diversity. Synergy between affirmative action and diversity is critical in breaking the self-defeating recruitment-oriented cycle (Thomas, 1990). Without the benefit of such synergy, the cycle of frustration, dormancy, and stagnation repeats itself as women and minorities plateau or simply leave. Figure 1 depicts the interrelationship between affirmative action and diversity as well as how diversity sustains the affirmative action process.

FIGURE 1
The Interrelationship of Affirmative Action and Diversity

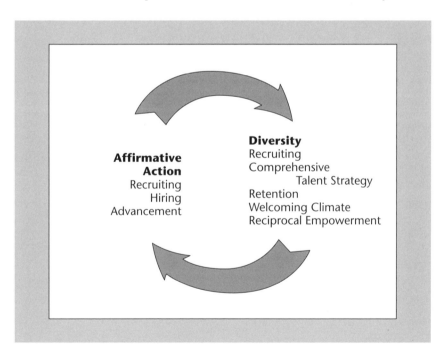

Source: Antokoviak, 2004.

Citing the limitations of affirmative action in sustaining diversity, Thomas (1990) identifies the affirmative action cycle as a self-defeating, recruitment-oriented cycle comprising six stages: (1) problem recognition (we need minorities and women); (2) intervention (affirmative action recruitment); (3) great expectations (new visible role models hired); (4) frustration (stagnation of minorities and women); (5) dormancy (a silent front is presented to the outside world); and (6) crisis (outside intervention leading back to the problem recognition phase). Once minorities and women leave the organization, the cycle of affirmative action repeats itself starting with step one at substantial cost to the institution.

In support of this insight, a survey of faculty in 487 universities and colleges in eight Midwestern states revealed not only a continuing pattern of underrepresentation of minority faculty but also a climate that reflects racial and ethnic bias toward those faculty (Turner, Myers, Samuel, and Creswell, 1999). Minority faculty identified common problems, among them the expectation of needing to work harder than others and the sense of being constantly scrutinized and in the spotlight. The study also highlights issues raised by different ethnic groups. African Americans most frequently mentioned concerns about being both hypervisible and invisible. Asian Americans felt pressure to absorb discrimination in silence. Latino faculty spoke of cultural isolation and overwork (Turner, Myers, Samuel, and Creswell, 1999).

Although affirmative action has generated some modest changes in the hiring of minorities and women in higher education, it still represents only an institutional starting point. According to Thomas (1990), affirmative action "gets the new fuel into the tank.... Something else will have to get them [minorities and women] in the drivers' seat" (p. 109). Once minorities and women are hired, the support mechanisms that assist their progress and success are critical because "the notion that cream will rise to the top is nonsense. Cream gets pulled or pushed to the top" (Thomas, 1990, p. 114).

To break the self-defeating affirmative action turnover cycle, sustained institutional attention is required to foster a climate that promotes reciprocal empowerment. Absent active institutional support, minorities and women can quickly become frustrated, silenced, or blocked by administrative and behavioral barriers. Although affirmative action may attempt to bring minorities and women into the pipeline, higher education leaders today face the challenge of creating an environment that fosters the conditions for reciprocal empowerment for women and minorities in the workplace.

The Impact of Supreme Court Decisions and Roads to the Future

Recent Supreme Court decisions relating to the admissions process in higher education have reaffirmed the educational value of diversity on college campuses while requiring that programs be "narrowly tailored" on the issue of race. These decisions do not affect the employment arena or the existing affirmative action requirements for employers who are federal contractors. Although the 2003 Supreme Court decisions in *Grutter* v. *Bollinger* (539 U.S. 306 [2003]) and *Gratz* v. *Bollinger* (539 U.S. 244 [2003]) dealt only with admissions, they underscore the Court's change in focus to an emphasis on diversity.

This focus evolved from the claim of reverse discrimination that arose most prominently in *Regents of the University of California* v. *Bakke* (438 U.S. 265 [1978]). In *Bakke* Supreme Court Justice Lewis F. Powell Jr. argued that universities need the right to select students who will contribute to the "robust exchange of ideas" to fulfill their mission (*Regents* v. *Bakke,* cited in Post and Rogin, 1998, p. 15). At the same time, the Court found the University of California at Davis Medical School's affirmative action admissions program unconstitutional in reserving places based on race and ethnicity alone. This opinion created a delicate balance, as it upheld the value of diversity in higher education yet destabilized academic affirmative action plans based on racial and ethnic preferences (Post and Rogin, 1998).

Continuing this line of thought, Supreme Court Justice Sandra Day O'Connor in *Grutter* v. *Bollinger* articulated the importance of fostering diversity in the student body and having a critical mass of minority students. Writing for the five-person majority, she found the Law School's admissions program to be acceptable from a constitutional perspective because it is narrowly tailored and considers all elements of an admissions application, including race, in a flexible manner (O'Connor, 2003).

With respect to the University of Michigan's undergraduate admissions criteria, in *Gratz* v. *Bollinger* the Supreme Court rejected the petitioners' assertion that diversity cannot constitute a compelling state interest (Crosby, 2004). At the same time Justice Rehnquist, writing for the Court majority, found that the admissions system used for undergraduates was unconstitutional, as the use of race was not narrowly tailored in its effort to achieve educational diversity. As a result the Court found that the policy violates the Equal Protection Clause of the Fourteenth Amendment of the Constitution.

In the late 1990s, a movement began toward diversity in colleges and universities that has been interpreted by some scholars as dismantling the apparatus of the civil rights era and replacing it with the concept of diversity (Myers, 1997). Ironically, emphasis on the value of diversity in the educational environment as reflected in these Supreme Court decisions can unintentionally mask or obscure the still unattained and much needed progress toward inclusion of underrepresented groups in the higher education workplace. By diffusing the focus to the broad palette of diversity, attention may be unwittingly diverted from the pressing and still unmet needs of minorities and women for greater inclusion and empowerment. Diversity can in effect become a smoke screen for eliminating affirmative action and focused efforts to assist underrepresented minorities (Myers, 1997). Diversity programs can be seen as a substitute for affirmative action and its historic effort to remedy racial underrepresentation (Myers, 1997).

Justice Sandra Day O'Connor, writing the five-person majority decision in *Grutter* v. *Bollinger,* indicated that she expected race-conscious affirmative action admissions programs would not be needed in twenty-five years (O'Connor, 2003). From the standpoint of the employment arena, evidence based on past progress indicates that the underrepresentation of minorities in the workplace will not be remedied in a quarter century or addressed through diversity programs alone. In fact the statistics demonstrate that the attack on the cruel disease of discrimination that President John F. Kennedy launched a half century ago has only begun to erode the subtle forces of power, resistance, and domination referenced in the model of reciprocal empowerment. The slow progress in hiring members of underrepresented groups and lack of change in workplace demographics suggest that not only is affirmative action in employment needed but also more aggressive measures may be necessary to achieve adequate representation of minorities. If the issue of workplace representation for minorities is not addressed, the goal of diversity will remain an unfulfilled challenge in higher education.

From a historical perspective, diversity development can be understood as an evolutionary process, with affirmative action as a necessary precursor on the road to diversity and inclusion. Perspectives on the evolution of diversity both as a concept and as a transformative process will help illuminate the pivotal role of affirmative action in attaining diversity.

Stages in Developing Diversity

Diversity development in higher education has been described as an evolutionary process that involves movement from rather monocultural to inclusive environments (Gardenswartz and Rowe, 1994; Smith, 1995; Valverde, 1998). Valverde, for example, identifies five stages of diversity development. In the first stage, the *monocultural* campus is devoid of minority cultures. The *ethnocentric* campus (the second stage) has a dominant white culture but admits minorities. In the third stage, the *accommodating* campus modifies personnel policies to accommodate women and minorities. The *transitional* campus (the fourth stage) has limited pluralism, while at the fifth and final stage, the *transformed* campus is fully multicultural (Valverde, 1998). This evolutionary continuum provides a way of gauging the degree and depth to which diversity has been achieved on campus. In fact as shown by the workplace demographics in higher education today, many campuses still remain at the monocultural level.

According to Smith (1995), the concept of diversity has similarly evolved over time in several phases or dimensions as the perspective on diversity has broadened. She identifies four dimensions: (1) representation or the perceived need to include previously underrepresented groups; (2) climate and responses to intolerance that shift attention to the institutional behavior and practices impacting psychosocial environment; (3) educational and scholarly mission and the effort to broaden the curriculum and acknowledge groups that have not been acknowledged from an academic perspective; and (4) transformation as campuses embrace multiple perspectives in support of educating a diverse student body for participation in a pluralistic society. These phases or dimensions may evolve sequentially or be present simultaneously in a campus environment, but efforts to implement diversity have only begun when the institution has sufficiently diverse representation to involve the other three dimensions (Smith, 1995).

Affirmative action and its focus on attaining structural representation galvanize the diversity process. As a result, affirmative action has been and remains at the core of the issue of diversity (Smith, 1995). Without the external mandate supplied by affirmative action, pressure might not be exerted to increase representation of minorities and women through structural diversity. Yet clearly as a mechanism for attaining inclusion and empowerment as well as for influencing psychosocial environment, affirmative action alone is not sufficient to attain institutional transformation.

As the dimensions of diversity development reveal, institutional climate and culture are critical components in readiness for diversity. In fact the results of a faculty survey conducted by the Higher Education Research Institute in 2004–2005 with 40,670 respondents at 421 institutions found that only 33 percent of the faculty indicated a climate of respect for diverse values was "very descriptive" of their institution (Lindholm, Szelenyi, Hurtado, and Korn, 2005, p. 17). Further, the perception of the existence of racial conflict on campus was substantially higher for African American and Latino faculty than for white and Native Hawaiian/Pacific Islander faculty (Lindholm, Szelenyi, Hurtado, and Korn, 2005). These results indicate that the climate and culture of an institution need to be receptive to diversity so that diversity efforts can be sustained and institutionalized rather than fragmented and transitory.

The Role of Culture and Climate

In moving toward diversity and inclusion, the culture and climate of an institution must be prepared to support representation before the later stages or dimensions of diversity can be attained. Leadership is the sine qua non in building representation and ensuring that the culture of the institution values and affirms diversity. Affirmative action programs are most successful when the institution unequivocally supports its principles, beginning with higher administration and pervading the entire institutional structure (Blackwell, 1996). Thus clarification of the meaning of culture and climate in institutional contexts is helpful in understanding the change effort that is needed. Further, higher education itself must be understood as one of the primary forces shaping the culture of society (Ropers-Huilman, 2003).

In each institutional context, individuals work together in community to carry out the work of the college or university and by their actions create a distinctive culture particular to that institution. In this respect, no formal rules or guidelines explain "the norms, goals, tacit sanctions, expectations, habits, and pressures that drive actual decisions; these live only in the human community that is the enterprise, and are continually reinforced by the actions of that community" (Senge, 2000b, p. 76). Institutions of higher education are living entities that literally reflect the attributes of the community and how they are translated into action daily.

Researchers have concluded that the culture of the college or university is the medium through which behavior is transmitted and interpreted. The culture in higher education has been described as an invisible tapestry that provides an "interpretive framework for understanding and appreciating events and actions ... rather than as a mechanism to influence or control behavior" (Kuh and Whitt, 1988, p. 3).

Divergent views on the word "culture" suggest on the one hand that it reflects deeply embedded values that are not easily changed or shaped and that encapsulate an organization's distinctive character (Peterson and Spencer, 1990) as well as more contemporary views such as that of Brockbank (2004) that the culture is the "collective hard-wiring" that translates ways of thinking into common ways of behaving. According to Brockbank, the cultural agenda is the most important agenda, as culture executes organizational strategy, meets marketplace needs, and determines the kind of organizations hired. From this perspective, the demands of the global workplace can no longer wait for slow and gradual cultural change (Brockbank, 2004).

Culture can also be understood as "the accumulated shared learning of a given group, covering behavioral, emotional, and cognitive elements of the group members' total psychological functioning" (Schein, 1992, p. 10). In this sense, the approach to cultural change is critical in overcoming behavioral barriers. Culture is normative because it governs how new members are introduced to the culture and shown the correct ways to act, think, and approach problems (Schein, 1992). The hegemonic process of cultural domination that is accomplished through the consent of those who are disempowered reveals how culture functions in a normative capacity. Organizational culture directly affects the differential allocation of power among diverse groups, as the ideologies inherent in the culture determine which behaviors and results will be rewarded (Ragins, 1995).

The word "climate" has been used to describe "common patterns of important dimensions of organizational life or its members' perceptions of attitudes toward these dimensions" (Peterson and Spencer, 1990, p. 7). As the word suggests, climate fluctuates, is more transient, and can reflect shorter-term changes. The study of "climate" has been used more recently to identify more complex psychological dimensions of the environment such as the notion of a "chilly climate" with its impact on the exclusion of women and minorities.

Different subcultures exist for faculty and administrative staff. In essence, faculty and administrative worlds function semi-independently and are driven by different rules and norms. Although the faculty and administrative worlds intersect and have a common locus or center, these subcultures are differentiated by significantly different terms and conditions of employment, professional expectations, educational preparation, and types of employment protection. Although the two subcultures may be congruent at certain points, the framework and ground rules are fundamentally different. Despite these variances, administrative and behavioral barriers may manifest themselves in similar ways.

In-depth diversity demands conceptual identification and explicit recognition of barriers to diversity in the culture of an institution; a high level of scrutiny in detecting these internal barriers; leadership to overcome negative stereotypes and promote the reciprocal empowerment of minorities and women in the workplace; and the institutionalization of administrative processes and programs that improve and sustain a culture of true diversity.

Identification of culture and climate and their relation to diversity goals in achieving institutional diversity naturally leads to consideration of the nature of twenty-first-century barriers to inclusion. Just as the concept of diversity has evolved over time, forms of discrimination have also changed.

Walking the Talk: Lip Service or Real Gains?

Beyond the initial hurdle of hiring, the challenges for institutions of higher education today have intensified. The playing field has gradually shifted: discrimination has changed from overt forms to covert or everyday forms (de la Luz Reyes and Halcon, 1988; Deitch and others, 2003; Feagin and McKinney, 2003; Kessler, Mickelson, and Williams, 1999; Scheurich and Young, 2002). The psychological and behavioral aspects of discrimination have now emerged as the most potent and powerful barriers to participation and empowerment. These psychological barricades are manifested in management practices and behaviors that undermine trust and respect such as ignoring individuals or even resorting to psychological intimidation or bullying. Given the stringent context of federal discrimination law, the new forms of discrimination are by necessity subtle and often difficult to pinpoint. The overt signs and signals that marked past unlawful discrimination and that the courts have curtailed are now essentially a relic. The covert nature of discrimination now makes it more difficult to pursue legal remedies.

The physiological effects of behavioral oppression and the creation of stress among women and minorities are factors that can lead to chronic illness and disease. A direct link has been shown between stress, the deleterious impact of continually activated stress responses, and the onset of stress-related disease (Sapolsky, 1992).

What then are the real measures of progress if we can no longer rely on simple hiring statistics or the absence of overt discrimination? How can diversity practitioners and higher education leaders translate visionary statements on diversity into practical, organizational realities?

One of the first steps in the process of raising awareness is to understand the ways in which subtle psychological discrimination is manifested. By increasing awareness of the presence of subtle forms of discrimination, higher education leaders can begin to develop a new set of barometers to gauge organizational pressures. Some of these measures may be qualitative and involve fostering a welcoming climate and facilitating reciprocal communication. Others may be quantitative such as turnover statistics, retention rates, and promotion statistics. These assessments will assist higher education leaders in designing effective strategies to increase organizational sensitivity and enhance the participation of minorities and women.

To be successful, *affirmative action and diversity* programs need to be strategic partners—protagonists joined in the effort to improve the demographic makeup of the workforce, strengthen retention of minorities and women, and foster a welcoming climate. Affirmative action's focus on monitoring and compliance is only an initial phase to be replaced by efforts to increase the potential for reciprocal empowerment.

As the history of limited enforcement has revealed, compliance with affirmative action goals and timetables is governed essentially with carrots and not sticks. The slow progress of attaining representation for minority group members demonstrates the fact that affirmative action has not yielded the needed representation so that diversity efforts can proceed. Because affirmative action has not yet achieved structural representation of minorities in the workforce, it still must address this fundamental issue to enable institutions of higher learning to progress toward the later phases of diversity.

As a result, new models must be developed to strengthen rewards and recognition of managerial excellence in building representation in the workforce, fostering diversity, and creating a climate in which reciprocal empowerment is the norm. Further, in moving from lip service to real gains, organizational strategies and processes need to focus on the reduction and elimination of the subtle psychological and behavioral forms of discrimination that will be examined in the next chapter. Without institutional commitment to sufficient representation of minorities and a climate that nurtures reciprocal empowerment, the achievement of diversity will remain illusory and elusive.

On the Way to Diversity: Psychological and Behavioral Barriers

I am an invisible man. I am invisible, understand, simply because people refuse to see me. When they approach me, they see only my surroundings, themselves, or figments of their imagination—indeed everything and anything except me.

—Ralph Ellison
Invisible Man, 1995 [1947], p. 3

A S FORMS OF MODERN RACISM have become more subtle and less overt in workplace settings, behavioral and psychological barriers have replaced more blatant forms of discrimination. Nonetheless, the striking invisibility and voicelessness of marginalized groups captured in the words of Ralph Ellison a half century ago find their contemporary parallel in the words of law professor Patricia Williams (1991): "They do not see me. I could force my presence, the real me contained in those eyes, on them, but I would be smashed in the process. If I deflect, if I move out of the way, they will never know I existed" (p. 23).

A new kind of invisibility, however, characterizes twenty-first-century discrimination. With the emergence of subtle forms of discrimination, the challenge for university leaders and administrators today is to recognize and make visible the invisible forms of discrimination. These forms of discrimination can affect the efforts of universities to retain diverse talent, sustain institutional excellence and quality, and maintain competitive advantage through the contributions of diverse faculty and staff. Increasing evidence identifies the severe marginalization experienced by racial and ethnic minority faculty in everyday social and professional interactions when they experience being isolated, unwelcome, unwanted, underemployed, unappreciated, and underrespected (Johnsrud, 1996; Turner and Myers, 2000). Unless diversity is managed effectively, minorities may feel like interlopers in the workplace who are sometimes viewed as the "ideal scapegoat" when their assumption of power and authority "is considered shocking and militant" (Cross, 1992, p. 30).

Only recently have scholars begun to explore the impact of subtle discrimination in the academic workplace in relation to health effects. One study of the academic workplace found that women and minorities report a high degree of stress resulting from subtle discrimination, with nonwhite women reporting levels at five times the rate reported by white males (Dey, 1994). Another study of stress in a land-grant university revealed that women faculty experience more work-related stress than their male counterparts (Smith, Anderson, and Lovrich, 1995). Other research suggests that perceived discrimination contributes to employee outcomes (job satisfaction, morale, work tension) beyond other work stressors (Sanchez and Brock, 1996).

This chapter first introduces terminology that describes contemporary behavioral discrimination based on research findings drawn largely from social psychology and social justice theory. These constructs provide a concrete contemporary vocabulary for describing behavioral forms of discrimination in the workplace. Through a brief exploration of the psychology of those who may knowingly or unknowingly serve as the agents of oppression, the potential of creating a new critical pedagogy of whiteness is described. Next, it reviews research findings that document how the internalization of oppression affects the self-esteem of women and minorities as well as the growing evidence of the physiological impact of discrimination. Knowledge and understanding of behavioral barriers and their effects on employees' performance is critical to the development of institutionwide strategies that address subtle forms of discrimination.

Psychosocial Discrimination and Attributional Ambiguity

The ambiguity that characterizes covert forms of contemporary discrimination presents singular challenges to minorities and women, as avoidance replaces face-to-face discriminatory speech. In this context, "the victims are the ones we talk *about* but avoid talking to" (Graumann and Wintermantel, 1989, p. 188). From a general perspective, psychosocial barriers involve forms of marginalization that are expressed through avoidance and distancing, microincursions, stereotyping, delegitimization, devaluation, and exclusion (Deitch and others, 2003; Graumann and Wintermantel, 1989; Westhues, 2004; Wylie, 1995). Because behavioral signals have assumed greater importance in the environment of subtle discrimination, the absence or avoidance of communication now reveals the existence of aversive, ambivalent attitudes (Graumann and Wintermantel, 1989).

Targets of subtle discrimination are often uncertain as to how to interpret ambivalent behavior and, as a result, experience what has been termed "attributional ambiguity" (Crocker, Vole, Test, and Major, 1991). Adding to the confusion, attitudes toward stigmatized groups may occasionally reflect feelings of sympathy by majority group members as well as the desire to avoid the appearance of prejudice (Crocker, Vole, Test, and Major, 1991).

Just as critical to an understanding of contemporary workplace discrimination is the psychology of those individuals who knowingly or unknowingly serve as the "agents of oppression" through the perpetuation of social stereotypes and acceptance of the legacy of privilege.

Psychology of the Agents of Oppression

As discussed earlier, the terminology developed over the last decade by social justice theorists provides a conceptual foundation for understanding the psychology of the agents of oppression who knowingly or unknowingly exercise unfair advantage over target groups (Hardiman and Jackson, 1997). The construct of "privilege" derives directly from membership in the dominant group and refers to the legacy of material and psychological privilege as well as the psychological freedom that derives from membership in this group (Goodman, 2001).

Denial of the existence of oppression is an option for members of privileged groups, as this denial has little effect on their social identities and even on daily realities. As part of the system of privilege, members of dominant groups inherit or carry on the legacy of what has been described as internalized supremacy or domination (Goodman, 2001; Hardiman and Jackson, 1997). Because awareness of one's social identity is not necessary for members of dominant groups, members of privileged groups tend to view themselves as unique individuals whose success or failure is determined by their own merits rather than through their position in the dominant social group (Goodman, 2001).

Recognition of oppression by members of the majority group does not mean asking members of the dominant culture to reject whiteness or assume guilt for past injustices (Rodriguez, 1998). Rather, because identity is evolving constantly and is being updated in light of encounters with history and cultural practices, individuals aware of the legacy of privilege can connect past injustices with present circumstances and understand how changes can be made (Rodriguez, 1998).

Why should individual members of dominant groups seek to disconnect themselves from past patterns of injustice and stereotyping? As Freire (1970) points out, the price of oppression for both subordinate and dominant groups is dehumanization. Oppression prevents both the oppressor and the oppressed from reaching their full humanity. In recent years, the concept of a critical pedagogy of whiteness has emerged as an important philosophical approach with the potential to free white identity from its cultural baggage as well as to reconceptualize and refashion this identity (Kincheloe and Steinberg, 1998).

Dimensions of Contemporary Workplace Discrimination

New constructs in the literature of social psychology illuminate how subtle forms of discrimination occur in contemporary workplace settings. These manifestations of discriminatory behavior are often covert, nonverbal, barely detectable, recurring, frequent, and cumulatively significant.

Microincursions and Microinequities

The term "everyday discrimination" refers to the frequency of the subtle dynamic of microincursions that has replaced more direct, egregious acts of discrimination (Deitch and others, 2003). Everyday discrimination can include a broad range of cultural practices and negative reactions to racial and gender characteristics that reflect gendered racism (St. Jean and Feagin, 1998). It occurs in pervasive and ambiguous ways—small incidents with large consequences that occur more frequently than severe forms of discrimination (Deitch and others, 2003). Micromessages are small, unspoken messages that when repeated have significant impact (Young, 2003). Microinequities erode organizations through "the power of the small" by sending devaluing messages that hinder performance and have a negative impact on employees' self-esteem (Young, 2003, p. 89). These events can have a cumulative effect on women and minorities, resulting in a decline in job satisfaction and well-being (Deitch and others, 2003).

Avoidance and Social Distance Theory

Research findings indicate avoidance is associated with negative attitudes toward marginalized groups. The phenomenon of social distance has been documented in the context of search, screening, and selection processes (Young and Fox, 2002). For example, an extensive study of the screening process occurring before interviewing found significant differences in callback rates based on presumed race (Bertrand and Mullainathan, 2004). Applicants with white-sounding names got one callback for about ten resumes, whereas applicants with African American names received one callback for about fifteen resumes. The study concluded that a white-sounding name was equivalent to an additional eight years of experience on the resume (Bertrand and Mullainathan, 2004). In addition, none of the employers who explicitly stated that they were "Equal Opportunity Employers" or the 11 percent who were federal contractors appeared to treat African Americans more favorably. In fact, these employers had a greater racial gap in callback rates, reflecting a significant disparity between rhetoric and hiring practices (Bertrand and Mullainathan, 2004).

Another form of avoidance links physical distance expressed through nonverbal behavior toward an individual with negative attitudes toward that individual. For example, in experimental interviews conducted with black and white interviewees who were students at Princeton University, more positive attitudes were found to be associated with closer direct eye contact, forward lean, more direct shoulder orientation, and closer interpersonal distance. Similarly, attitudes toward conventionally stigmatized persons suggest nonverbal behaviors of avoidance, including greater distances and terminating interviews sooner (Word, Zanna, and Cooper, 2000).

Aversive Racism

The term "aversive racism" illuminates the ambiguity in modern everyday discrimination and refers to white Americans with egalitarian values who support public policies that promote racial equality while holding negative feelings and beliefs about blacks (Dovidio, Gaertner, and Bachman, 2001; Gaertner and Dovidio, 2000). In situations that threaten to expose their underlying negative attitudes, aversive racists may overreact and amplify positive behavior in the attempt to reconcile negative feelings with their own self-image. At other times, "the underlying negative portion of their attitudes is expressed, but in subtle, rationalizable ways" (Gaertner and Dovidio, 2000, p. 289).

Aversive racism can result in a subtle backlash that produces greater bias against higher-status African Americans who pose a greater threat, whether symbolically or directly, to the dominance of the majority group (Dovidio, Gaertner, and Bachman, 2001). In this sense, aversive racism provides a psychological explanation for the phenomenon of the "glass ceiling" (Dovidio, Gaertner, and Bachman, 2001).

Threat and Delegitimization

Because behavioral signals are an important clue to the existence of subtle psychosocial discrimination in the work environment, the phenomenon of distancing and separation involved in behavioral discrimination takes its most extreme form in delegitimization (Bar-Tal, 1989). Delegitimization occurs when groups or individuals are stereotyped into highly negative social categories—a process by which differences are accentuated, distorted, and amplified. This extreme form of negative typecasting and polarization differs only in degree from more ordinary forms of discrimination. Delegitimization can occur unconsciously through acceptance of stereotypes prevalent in the culture (Bar-Tal, 1989).

The phenomena of threat and delegitimization are inextricably linked. The more threatened a group, the more it will attempt to delegitimize the threatening group. A threat to the group's sense of security can activate the process of delegitimization that serves as a coping mechanism for the threatened group (Bar-Tal, 1989). Devaluing groups is easier when differences are greater or more obvious such as when differences are based on physical appearance and boundaries can be drawn more readily. The less one group values the other, the simpler the process of delegitimization. Delegitimizing labels are more easily applied because no dramatic change in perception is required, only reinforcement of preexisting beliefs (Bar-Tal, 1989).

Workplace Mobbing

An extreme form of delegitimization is "workplace mobbing," a term used to describe a collective effort "to exclude, punish and humiliate a targeted worker" that has been documented in reports from a number of universities (Westhues, 2004, p. 4). Clues to mobbing and the effort to exclude others can range from prior marginalization of the worker, unanimity of opinion, a popular high-achieving target, and secrecy to resistance to external review, lack of due process, fuzzy charges, backbiting, and impassioned rhetoric (Westhues, 2004). Although the connection to race and gender is not specifically made in this research, the distancing, avoidance, and ambiguous attitudes described in contemporary forms of workplace discrimination can create the context for this form of delegitimization.

Second-Generation Obstacles and Multiple Jeopardy Theory

Although first-generation barriers were formal structural barriers preventing entry to institutions addressed through direct governmental intervention, second-stage barriers typically involve subjective, interpersonal, situational, and even superficially nonracial elements such as closed or unfriendly verbal and nonverbal communication and failure to provide assistance (Pettigrew and Martin, 1987).

Once hired, minority employees face social psychological obstacles that are captured in the notion of "jeopardy." Triple-jeopardy theory refers to the impact of negative racial stereotypes, the solo role, and the token role of the supposedly incompetent affirmative action hire (Pettigrew and Martin, 1987). The compounding of jeopardy in academe has also been described in terms of the status of being both female and a minority (see Fontaine and Greenlee, 1993; Graves, 1990; Lindsay, 1994).

Research findings suggest that solos, during the initial stages of their employment, are viewed in terms of exaggerated and extreme evaluations—either "golden" or "hopelessly doomed to failure" (Pettigrew and Martin, 1987, p. 57). After minorities and women pass the initial obstacles of recruitment and entry to an organization, the perceived threat to existing employees becomes more direct. The possibility of biased perception and evaluation of performance can actually increase after hiring. In fact, "there is considerable evidence that blacks—*particularly if they are high performers*—receive unfairly low performance evaluations" (Pettigrew and Martin, 1987, p. 60). The linking of unfairly low performance evaluations with high performance provides evidence of the presence of a perceived threat and the ensuing attempt at delegitimization. Multiple forms of jeopardy can result in extremely low or extremely high expectations and evaluations of minority employees (Pettigrew and Martin, 1987). One research study of female faculty and administrators reports that black females feel they must outthink, outperform, and outshine majority group colleagues to obtain legitimacy in the academy (Fontaine and Greenlee, 1993).

When minority and female faculty and administrators are perceived as a threat, the term "diversity backlash" describes how a "preemptive strike" can take place against the development of power by a minority group even before that group assumes power (Ragins, 1995). Diversity backlash may occur in both covert and overt forms and include stereotyping, exclusion, and belittling characteristics of minority group members (Ragins, 1995).

The isolation of minorities and women in organizational settings may be intensified by the fact that frequently the minority or woman employee is the only one in a position to realize that ambiguous microincursions are occurring. Nonracial or nonsexist reasons could be given to explain ambiguous incidents. Minority or women employees may be labeled as "oversensitive" or "touchy." As a result, second-generation forms of discrimination often remain invisible, even to its perpetrators (Pettigrew and Martin, 1987).

Self-Fulfilling Prophecy

One of the most prevalent of underlying assumptions about the performance of minorities and women is incompetence. The assumption of incompetence produces the potential for self-fulfilling prophecy because this behavioral barrier can undermine the performance of women and minorities and affect their self-esteem. The cyclical effect and interrelationship of expectation and performance in educational settings has been described in terms of "stereotype threat" in which a negative stereotype generates an emotional response that directly interferes with the performance of minorities (Steele, 1997).

Internalization: The Impact of Discrimination on Self-Esteem

Exploration of how the internalization of contemporary forms of oppression may affect the self-esteem of minorities and women will assist administrators and human resource professionals to build a workplace of choice in terms of employee performance, job satisfaction, morale, and productivity. The impact of systemic discrimination is not restricted to the workplace but may emanate from the workplace to disrupt the affected individual's life and destabilize the family environment (Feagin and McKinney, 2003). As a result, awareness of the wide-ranging effects of discriminatory behavior is crucial in the development of proactive institutional strategies to overcome behavioral barriers.

When they unconsciously become their own oppressors, minorities and women may inappropriately interpret instances of everyday discrimination in terms of their own personal and dispositional inadequacies rather than in terms of situational and contextual factors. This inappropriate translation can in turn create a cycle of self-imposed oppression and self-blame. To cope with perceived barriers, minorities and women can benefit from a deeper understanding of their own responses to subtle discrimination.

Because the same behavior can be interpreted differently based on the race of the originator of the action, minorities and women must exercise additional caution in the workplace and even overcompensate for existing stereotypes. For example, Gregory (2003) writes of her experiences being a black female professor in terms of the criticism she received for not being rigorous or tough enough, despite the fact that her grade distribution and class assignments were similar to those of other professors.

An important research finding reveals that appropriately attributing negative outcomes to prejudice can serve a self-protective function for those who are the targets of discriminatory behavior and offset emotional reactions to these behaviors (Crocker, Vole, Test, and Major, 1991). In other words, the stigmatized subject's self-esteem is not affected negatively or as negatively if the individual is able to attribute outcomes appropriately to perceived racism (Crocker, Vole, Test, and Major, 1991). The predictability of negative stimuli may also enable the lowering of stress (Sapolsky, 1998). Conversely, even when positive feedback is delivered, if racism is suspected, self-esteem has been shown to suffer (Crocker, Vole, Test, and Major, 1991). Mechanisms that protect or buffer the self-esteem of members of stigmatized groups from external prejudice include attributing negative outcomes to prejudice, comparing outcomes with the outcomes of other group members, and valuing attributes in which the group excels while devaluing those in which it does not (Crocker and Major, 1989).

How the self-esteem of minorities and women is affected by discrimination is a complex phenomenon, as research suggests that global feelings of self-worth may differ from other subdimensions of self-esteem such as dimension-specific self-esteem and racial self-esteem (Crocker and Major, 1989). As a result, evaluations of the self on academic ability, social skills, and physical appearance are correlated with global feelings of self-worth but are "neither conceptually nor empirically identical" (Crocker and Major, 1989, p. 608). This finding suggests that even if, for example, academic performance is high, self-esteem in this dimension may not correlate with global self-esteem.

Minimizing discrimination appears to vary among ethnic groups and between the sexes. Women may be more inclined to internalize negative feedback on achievement-related tasks than men and to respond with sadness and shame rather than overt aggression or anger (Bettencourt and Miller, 1996, cited in Ruggiero and Taylor, 1997). In addition, a correlation has been found between perceived discrimination and depression among women (Corning, 2002). Asian American students were found to have a greater tendency to minimize discrimination and blame failures on the quality of their own performance when compared with members of other minority groups (Ruggiero and Taylor, 1997).

Given the complexity of theories regarding self-esteem, further research will undoubtedly continue to clarify the impact of perceived discrimination on self-esteem and domains. From a practical perspective, the self-esteem of minorities and women can be affected by external circumstances that may undermine the overall stability of global self-esteem. The cumulative effect of many instances of perceived discrimination could override the ability to contextualize specific instances of situational discrimination.

The Physiological Impact of Perceived Discrimination: A Scientific Perspective

As discussed earlier, the impact of discrimination on minorities and women is clearly linked in recent research to increased levels of stress. Perceived discrimination results in heightened "psychological and physiological stress responses that are influenced by constitutional, social-demographic, psychological and behavioral factors and coping responses. Over time, these stress responses influence health outcomes" (Clark, Anderson, Clark, and Williams, 1999, p. 806).

Stress must be understood from a holistic perspective as comprising environmental, psychological, and biological dimensions (Cohen, Kessler, and Gordon, 1995, cited in Allison, 1998). Further, stressors have a cumulative impact. As a result, individuals experiencing multiple stressful events have a higher likelihood that the pathology will be intensified, with increased odds for major depression or generalized anxiety disorder (Kessler, Mickelson, and Williams, 1999). In particular, prolonged stress can heighten susceptibility to a number of autoimmune diseases such as diabetes and myopathy and can result in exacerbation of cardiovascular disease, digestive disorders, and neurological disease (Sapolsky, 1998). Continuous activation of the stress response causes the individual to tire more easily and experience fatigue, and it can trigger the breakdown of proteins in the muscles without allowing the muscles to rebuild (Sapolsky, 1992).

Researchers have identified the role of racial discrimination in shaping patterns of blood pressure and influencing adult mortality among African Americans through comparison of differences in blood pressures among blacks and whites (Cooper, 1993; Feagin and McKinney, 2003; Krieger and Sidney, 1996). Hypertension has been shown to increase death rates by 25 percent among blacks and 10 percent among whites (Cooper, 1993). Because direct evidence that indicates genetic differences relating to hypertension is lacking, lower life expectancy and higher death rates among blacks lend credence to a link among life experiences, race, and health (Cooper, 1993). Systolic blood pressure was found to reach higher levels among black women who typically responded to unfair treatment by keeping it to themselves and accepting it, compared with individuals who tried to do something about it and talked to others about it (Krieger and Sidney, 1996).

The impact of repeated microincursions combined with instances of blatant discrimination in the workplace can create a continual draw on the psychological resources of women and minorities. The stress of institutionalized racism affects the store of energy each individual has to cope with everyday life (Feagin and McKinney, 2003). As a retired black psychologist explains, if each individual is given [one hundred] units of energy to live out his or her life, a black person "uses fifty percent the same way a white man does, dealing with what the white man has [to deal with], so he has fifty percent left. But he uses twenty-five percent fighting being black, [with] all the problems in being black and what it means" (Feagin and Sikes, 1994, cited in Feagin and McKinney, 2003, p. 296).

The differential use of psychological resources by women and minorities is in essence a double-edged sword. If the individual can sustain the challenges that accumulate over a long period of time, he or she may be better equipped to deal with discrimination. Yet the physical toll from stress and stress-related disease can be substantial. As a result, strategies that assist women and minorities to cope with psychological and behavioral barriers in the higher education workplace can offset and buffer the impact of subtle forms of discrimination, reduce job-related stress, and assist in meeting challenges of the workplace.

Recognition of psychological and behavioral barriers has implications for higher education in terms of the development of institutional policy and programs that seek to eliminate subtle forms of race and sex discrimination, especially in promotion, tenure, workload distribution, and other administrative processes (Tack and Patitu, 1992; Dey, 1994). To create an improved climate for diversity, campus leaders must make a conscious effort to achieve a campus climate that supports diversity and to rid the campus of its exclusionary past (Hurtado, Milem, Clayton-Pedersen, and Allen, 1999). Development of institutional strategies and programs that raise awareness of psychological and behavioral barriers will improve the retention of minorities and women, foster a climate of increased receptivity to diversity, and lay the groundwork for a workplace that supports reciprocal empowerment.

On the Way to Diversity: Organizational Barriers

*What happens when prejudice is codified in operating assumptions
about minorities' business sense, work ethics, or ability to manage
white staff? ... Minority executives told us again and again that
for them, race meant that they had to be better and do more than
their white peers. They view overachievement as the only response
to the unstated questions of whether or not they deserve all that
came to them. For them, it's not enough to be the best once. They
have to—need to—prove themselves every time they start a new
job. The tax of prejudice is time.*

—Thomas and Gabarro, 1999, p. 74

THIS CHAPTER FOCUSES ON ten key organizational barriers in the
higher education workplace that can be used to help gauge progress in
enhancing the participation and inclusion of minorities and women. These
barriers, like behavioral forms of discrimination, may be invisible, difficult to
pinpoint, covert, and cumulative in impact. The organizational barriers range
from clear process-oriented barriers such as hiring and promotion to those that
occur in less traceable ways yet obstruct career progress and success in administrative procedures. Less perceptible organizational barriers such as isolation,
lack of mentoring, lack of access to social networks, and perceptions of
tokenism lead to marginalization, increased stress, decreased morale, and an
experience of the higher education environment for minorities and women
that differs from that for white male peers (Cooper and Stevens, 2002b;

Johnsrud, 1996; Park, 1996; Perna, 2005; Tack and Patitu, 1992; Thomas and Hollenshead, 2001; Thompson and Dey, 1998; Van Ummersen, 2005; Winkler, 2000).

Unlike formal organizational barriers, informal barriers are less likely to receive institutional attention. Without the active and persistent intervention of leadership, however, these barriers may persist unchecked in the organizational culture and block achievement of the goal of reciprocal empowerment. Moreover, if female and minority faculty and administrators are unaware of how informal barriers operate, they will lack the institutional know-how needed to surmount them to succeed in formal institutional processes. The chapter also provides an overview of major sources of workplace power in the university setting, as the interplay of these forces directly affects support for diversity in institutional culture.

Formal and Informal Organizational Barriers

The ten organizational barriers to diversity directly affect how workplace power is perceived, disseminated, and shared. From a holistic perspective, an organization's cultural, structural, and behavioral levels function interdependently, and a change in one domain affects the other levels (Ragins, 1995). Formal and informal organizational barriers can reflect behaviors in an organization or deep-rooted cultural assumptions that are enacted in the context of workplace power. These barriers include both formal and informal ways in which the complex interplay of cultural and behavioral forces can surface in work settings and affect administrative processes. The barriers, which are not presented in order of importance, can be present simultaneously and have damaging effects of significant magnitude.

Hiring

The discussion of affirmative action earlier in the monograph provides historical perspective on efforts to increase the structural representation of minorities and women in higher education through the hiring process. Historically, colleges and universities have a demonstrated record of exclusion of minorities in both the student body and the faculty and staff. Despite articulation of the goals of enlightenment, excellence, and tolerance, American universities have frequently been "centers of racial exclusion, animosity, and discrimination," reflecting a Eurocentric vision of the world (Feagin, Vera, and Imani, 1996, p. 19). Statistics on the hiring of black faculty members indicate historic patterns of discrimination. In 1940, not one of 330 black doctorate holders in the United States taught at a white university (Feagin, Vera, and Imani, 1996). Twenty years later, only three hundred (3.5 percent of total full-time faculty) were employed in white institutions (Jackson, 1991). A large number of black faculty continue to be employed in traditionally black institutions and to be less represented in the highest ranked academic institutions (Cross and Slater, 2002). By 2003, although the number of black faculty had increased significantly, in research universities black faculty members still held only 3.6 percent of all tenure-track positions (U.S. Department of Education, 2003a).

Evidence of the impact of gender on faculty hiring was noted in one of the first comparative studies undertaken in 1999 with a sample of 238 male and female academic psychologists (Steinpreis, Anders, and Ritzke, 1999). Both male and female psychologists were found significantly more likely to hire a male job applicant and rate the applicant higher on research, teaching, and service contributions than a female with an identical record (Steinpreis, Anders, and Ritzke, 1999). Similarly, the paucity of women and virtual nonexistence of minority women in the science and engineering faculties of the fifty top-rated research universities reflect gender disparities in hiring decisions (Nelson and Rogers, 2004). For example, despite the higher percentage of women Ph.D. recipients in the biological sciences (44.7 percent), the percentage of women hired (30.2 percent) was lower than male doctoral recipients (43.2 percent of earned doctorates), who represented 55.4 percent of assistant professors in the institutions studied (Nelson and Rogers, 2004). The lack of minority and women faculty in the sciences, mathematics, and engineering is of grave concern as the United States seeks to remain competitive in global research (Van Ummersen, 2005).

Promotion and Advancement

The twenty-first-century battleground for equalizing opportunities has shifted from hiring to promotion and advancement, based on a decline in discrimination claims related to hiring and a corresponding rise in claims related to promotion (Elliott and Smith, 2004). Dissatisfaction in the area of promotion, particularly in relation to slower rates of promotion for minority and women faculty, influences faculty turnover (Gregory, 2001; Tack and Patitu, 1992). Research indicates that minority faculty members find promotion and tenure procedures ambiguous and inequitably administered (Gregory, 2001). One study of 289 institutions reports that one of the greatest sources of stress for minority and women faculty members in four-year institutions is concerns about promotion (Thompson and Dey, 1998). In particular, areas in which African American faculty experience greater amounts of stress are promotion, time constraints, and overall stress (Thompson and Dey, 1998).

Talented individuals will not stay with an organization if their careers remain stalled or if they are marginalized. An accumulation of disadvantages in the career socialization process in higher education can lead to an unaccommodating culture that hinders the advancement of women and minorities and results in professional attrition (Marschke, Laursen, Nielsen, and Rankin, 2007).

In decisions about promotion, psychological closeness, the similar-to-me effect, and prior expectations have been proposed as factors influencing supervisory assessment of performance (Greenhaus and Parasuraman, 1993). These factors may have adverse impact on the advancement of minorities and women.

Lack of Support

Lack of organizational support influences the ability of minorities and women to be successful in their roles and may in fact cause them to be ineffective in their positions (Gregory, 2001; Patitu and Hinton, 2003). Withholding encouragement, minimizing accomplishments or damning with faint praise, and riding the emotional rollercoaster of occasional positive feedback in a context of general avoidance or indirect criticism are all examples of lack of support. Lack of support is the most elusive barrier because it is more subtle and difficult to detect.

Lack of support can be detected in evaluation processes when, for example, language is used to cast female faculty in a negative light by manipulating the "academic lexicon" to create and justify negative assessments (Winkler, 2000).

In this context, the vagueness of criteria may permit the interjection of personal biases that influence decisions about reappointment, tenure, and promotion (Winkler, 2000). Armed with the critical vocabulary and political know-how, ways can be found to delicately skew or justify predetermined negative appraisals. In another example, African American female administrators in one study reported lack of support in the form of budget constraints, denial of programming resources, and simply being ignored or isolated in the organization (Patitu and Hinton, 2003).

Failure to Empower and Include in Decision Making

The indicator of decision making is a litmus test that belies the mere presence in the institution of minority and women faculty and upper-level administrators. The absence of decision-making authority may be at variance with official titles or designations. Although women and minorities may receive high-ranking positions, they sometimes lack the authority associated with them and have less ability to influence the compliance of subordinates (Ragins, 1995). Minority faculty are unlikely to be able to be viable agents of leadership in higher education or in a position to change organizational distribution of power and privilege because they are outside the mainstream and must lead from the margins (Aguirre and Martinez, 2002).

Differing Expectations

The fifth barrier is applying differing expectations to minorities and women, resulting in a double standard and preferential treatment for nonminority employees in the workplace. For example, representative minority faculty in a study of fifty-five minority faculty in Midwestern colleges and universities identified the need to be twice as good as nonminority faculty and to exceed the performance of whites in similar situations while constantly under scrutiny (Turner and Myers, 2000).

One study of 1,167 faculty respondents at a Midwestern public research university reports that minority faculty women were least likely to report that their research was valued by colleagues, that colleagues asked their opinions on research ideas, and that colleagues used appropriate criteria to review their work (Thomas and Hollenshead, 2001). This research perspective counters the perception that minorities and women are given extra chances to succeed and instead underscores the differential standards that may be applied.

Stereotyping and Organizational Fit

The sixth administrative barrier is stereotyping and the perceived "fit" of women and minorities in the organization. The concept of "fit" can identify the degree to which women and minorities are marginalized in a given cultural environment (Aguirre, 2000). Women and minorities who are relegated to peripheral participation in the academic workplace or marginalized in certain roles have a "weak fit." This weak fit causes women and minorities to occupy "a niche in the academic workplace that is typified by their gender and/or minority status and promotes their image as 'tokens' or 'anomalies'" (Aguirre, 2000, p. 53). This niche can mean, in some instances, that research conducted by minority or women faculty on feminist or minority issues is devalued and considered outside the mainstream.

Fit can involve horizontal segregation such as the predominance of women and minorities in certain job classes and sectors of the organization (Wirth, 2001). This segregation occurs when the organizational pyramid has support staff on the bottom with women and minorities clustered in the lower ranks and women and minorities sparsely represented at the top of the pyramid in the more strategic, visible roles (Wirth, 2001).

A third application of the word "fit" takes place in administrative processes such as hiring and promotion when stereotyping affects how individuals are perceived to fit or not fit in the academic workplace. In this regard, a recent research study conducted in two major U.S. cities found that numerous employers admitted that when hiring, stereotypes about minority workers involving personality traits, attitudes, and behaviors had come into play (Feagin, 2001). Mediocre past performance by minority workers is often attributed to permanent variables such as personality, incompetence, and inadequate background, while for white males failure is attributed to transitory conditions like health (Lindsay, 1994).

As another example, the model minority concept applied to Asian Americans transforms seemingly positive characteristics into negative attributes (Wu, 1995). The stereotype reversal for Asian Americans occurs as follows:

"… [T]o be intelligent is to lack personality. To be hard-working is to be unfairly competitive. To be family-oriented is to be clannish, 'too ethnic,' and unwilling to assimilate" (Wu, 1995, p. 241). Stereotype reversal can affect organizational perceptions of the ability of Asian Americans to fit leadership roles rather than technical roles.

Stereotyping may involve the application of a differential assessment of capabilities based on preexisting biases. The same behavior that is seen as assertive and decisive in a man can be viewed as unpleasantly aggressive and controlling in a woman. Similarly, attention to detail by women administrators can be seen as the inability to engage in strategic thinking. For example, in one study a vice provost, when interviewed about her chances for becoming president, emphasized that women need to have greater accomplishments in financial and legal areas to be president, given the presumption that men have more business sense (Glazer-Raymo, 1999).

Lack of Mentoring and Access to Formal and Informal Networks
Mentoring and networks provide opportunities to access valuable informal information about how the organization functions. In an institution of higher education, mentors can uncover limited organizational resources, surface historical knowledge, and warn of potential minefields. Mentoring can prevent costly organizational missteps or mistakes that can derail careers or cause permanent career damage through a single, major mistake (Catalyst, 1999, cited in Kilian, Hukai, and McCarty, 2005).

At the same time, mentoring may not always be a viable alternative when the involvement of mentors will entail career risks by increasing vulnerability. For example, as one study at a public research university reports, mentoring is not normative for faculty because junior faculty hesitate to involve senior colleagues who may evaluate them in the future for tenure and promotion (Sands, Parson, and Duane, 1991).

Mentoring is not critical in terms of career guidance or psychosocial support (Tillman, 2001). Interviews with a sample of ten African American faculty from two predominantly white Midwestern research institutions suggest that whereas the professional guidance performed by a mentor in the tenure process may function well in cross-race situations, psychosocial support for minority faculty is sometimes sought from other minority faculty mentors (Tillman, 2001).

Countering the expectation that those who have experienced workplace barriers may naturally provide greater assistance to others, the phenomenon of the "queen bee syndrome" describes women who place more stringent expectations on other females and even align themselves with those against the advancement of other women because of the feeling that they have worked hard to reach a position of rank and other women should do the same (Snipes, Oswald, and Caudill, 1998). In addition, some women may not feel the need to assist others or may not realize the value of the mentoring relationship because they succeeded without it (Sands, Parson, and Duane, 1991). Other research suggests that willingness to mentor among women may be more likely to occur above the glass ceiling when risks to the visibility of a same-gender mentoring relationship decrease (Ragins, 1995).

In some instances, women faculty seeking to develop a mentoring relationship have reported the possibility of sexual harassment. In fact, 29 percent of the women faculty surveyed in a study of faculty in a Midwestern research university indicated that they had experienced sexual harassment from senior male colleagues. In addition, 59 percent of the women felt their work was underestimated and undervalued because of their sex (Sands, Parson, and Duane, 1991).

What types of networks are the most helpful for women and minorities? Research indicates that networks that are heterogeneous in three dimensions are the most effective: (1) functional diversity in terms of mentors, role models, and even potential mentees; (2) variety of position and location (both internally and externally to the organization); and (3) demographically mixed by age, race, gender, and culture (Thomas, 2001). When white mentors understand and acknowledge race as a potential barrier, minorities tend to advance farther (Thomas, 2001). To foster mentoring that acknowledges race-related barriers, a white mentor could, for example, publicly endorse the good ideas of his or her protégé and the value of his or her perspectives (Thomas, 2001).

Heterogeneous networks amplify the range of contacts and the specializations reflected in the network. In the higher education environment, networks can include faculty, staff, and administrators, as each perspective provides different organizational insights and expertise. As a result of the separate subcultures in the university environment, maintaining a mix of contacts allows for a rich combination of insights and understanding.

Isolation and Soloing

The eighth organizational barrier to diversity is isolation and solo roles in the workplace resulting from the lack of minorities and women. A study of 1,500 four-year colleges and universities reveals that the gender composition of the institution's workforce was more balanced when institutions had a higher proportion of women students and women administrators (Kulis, 1997). The importance of critical mass is also demonstrated in research indicating that women tend to receive lower performance evaluations when the proportion of women in a group is small (Sackett, DuBois, and Noe, 1991). Skewed situations are more likely to promote stereotyped evaluations with a potential for discriminatory impact, as noted by the American Psychological Association in its examination of *Price* v. *Waterhouse* (Sackett, DuBois, and Noe, 1991).

Without sufficient feedback, solo minority and female employees operate in a vacuum without the benefit of accurate feedback—much like a plane flying without a gyroscope (Pettigrew and Martin, 1987). As a result of the lack of an appropriate navigational system and radar screen, women and minorities may find it difficult to identify and overcome hidden behavioral and administrative barriers in an organization.

Tokenism

The ninth organizational barrier is tokenism; it involves the hiring of a single individual or a few isolated individuals to satisfy the institutional need for diversity among administrators or faculty. One of the main characteristics of tokenism is the assumption that the goal of diversity has been satisfied with the hiring of these few minorities or women who may in fact be marginalized and not empowered with organizational resources or decision-making capabilities. Tokenism is described in Kanter's analysis of white women in organizational settings (1977) who differ from the norm and experience a series of multiple disadvantages such as increased visibility and pressure to conform. Minority women may find it especially difficult to tell which type of tokenism (race or gender) is operating and may consequently experience multiple episodes of marginality in the academic workplace (Turner, 2002).

The Revolving Door

The last organizational barrier is an outcome of all the preceding barriers and results when behavioral, cultural, and organizational barriers obstruct the progress and success of minorities and women in the workplace and lead to the departure of these individuals from the workplace. Women and minority faculty members who do not reach tenure may have worked four to six years, received an unfavorable tenure evaluation, and be forced to leave (Gregory, 2001). As mentioned earlier, without proactive retention and support, the self-defeating recruitment-oriented cycle will continue (Thomas, 1990).

The ten organizational barriers identified in this section present positive opportunities for the development of focused strategies by institutional leadership. The next section further discusses the major constituencies in the academic workplace and provides an understanding of the environment in which effective diversity strategies can be initiated, implemented, and cultivated.

Workplace Power: Understanding the New Battleground

Research findings reveal that organizational inequality for women and minorities does not take the form of a simple boundary or glass ceiling at a certain level of the organization but instead increases in both *intensity* and *magnitude* at higher levels of power (Elliott and Smith, 2004; Wright and Baxter, 2000). Rather than an absolute glass ceiling that precludes any further progress of minorities and women, researchers found a *decreasing* probability of advancement of minorities relative to white men at higher levels of power in a multicity survey of urban inequality conducted from 1992 to 1994 (Elliott and Smith, 2004). The study also lends credence to Kanter's theory of homosocial reproduction that identifies the persistence of the social characteristics of organizations over time as a result of the selection and advancement of self-similar others in hiring and promotion (Kanter, 1977). For administrative positions, the higher the level of the position, the more difficult it is to specify the needed skills and abilities and the more amorphous selection criteria become (Johnsrud and Heck, 1994). This difficulty results in subjective assessments that may be affected more by similarity to self than by the needed skills for a given position (Johnsrud and Heck, 1994).

Workplace power in the context of public research universities is multifaceted, and the interrelationship of these dimensions of power can, in some settings, increase the probability of checks and balances in decision-making processes. Power dimensions in public research universities typically include several components: academic governance, the hierarchical campus-based administrative structure, a local board of trustees, unionized groups, departmental authority, and faculty or staff unions. A centralized chancellor's or president's office may retain oversight and authority in specified processes. Further, public research institutions must respond to legislative and executive governmental authority, and alumni and community networks can exercise influence on the decision-making process. Even when delegation of authority may occur, significant power still resides in the campus-based administrative hierarchy through the principal administrative officials (president, provost, vice presidents, deans) who exercise considerable authority over important aspects of university decision making (Hammond, 2004).

The following sections discuss these dimensions of workplace power in terms of their potential to assist in building a culture of diversity and inclusion.

Shared Governance

The concept of shared governance suggests an important source of power, an opportunity for the involvement of women and minority faculty, and potential links to goals for diversity in the research university. In particular, the American Association of University Professors' formal adoption of the "Statement on Government of Colleges and Universities" in 1966 clearly identifies the professoriat as having primary authority over curriculum matters as well as research and faculty status (American Association of University Professors, 1966). One of the measures that can be used to evaluate an institution's response to diversity is the extent to which minority faculty participate in governance activities and the incorporation of diversity issues into the curriculum (Aguirre and Martinez, 2002).

The traditional approach to shared governance relegated specific issues to specific constituencies, resulting in segmented decision making (Minor and Tierney, 2005). In contrast to this segmentation, Minor and Tierney propose a *cultural* framework for shared governance that links governance with quality and recognizes the role of governance in the institution's communicative and symbolic processes. The cultural framework for understanding shared governance represents one approach to linking diversity with institutional values and with quality.

In the continuing debate over the role of shared governance, the view that governance and culture need to be integrated spheres has particular value in our campuses' progressive evolution to greater diversity. By melding the cultural perspective with effective systems and finely calibrated structures, the concept of shared governance can support efforts to enhance inclusion in the institutional environment. The participation of minority faculty in governance can help define values and preferences and include competing viewpoints in the development of institutional policies (Aguirre and Martinez, 2002).

Academic Department Chairs

Although the vehicle for shared governance is the faculty senate and the established rules of governance, academic chairs as department leaders are important participants in the administrative power structure. They wield considerable influence by virtue of their academic standing, impact on academic personnel processes, and selection for leadership among academic peers. As managers or administrative leaders "on loan," their authority lies in credibility, persuasiveness, and influence rather than on formal power (Senge, 2000a, p. 283). Because culture shifts begin on a local level and are a result of everyday ways of doing things, the source of needed innovation in the university environment potentially centers on clusters of faculty and department chairs (Senge, 2000a). Department chairs play a critical role in the implementation of goals for diversity, particularly through faculty recruitment, hiring, and promotion. They are the bridge between the academic and administrative sides of the university structure.

Academic department chairs can empower untenured minority and women faculty by ensuring their involvement in departmental decision making and meetings (McDonough, 2002). In particular, opportunities to serve on departmental personnel appointment and review committees provide valuable learning opportunities regarding institutional policies for pretenure faculty (McDonough, 2002). In assisting pretenure faculty, chairs have discretion in determining individual faculty courseloads, sharing ways to mitigate the teaching preparation process, structuring mentoring experiences, and helping them become part of the academic community (McDonough, 2002).

Boards of Trustees

The role of the board of trustees varies with its power and influence. Some state systems may have a board of regents appointed by the governor and have local boards with considerably less power and influence. In examining the potential influence of boards of trustees, critics have found that in some cases trustees are reluctant to challenge the decision-making process and have as a result become increasingly irrelevant in the governance process (Schaefer, 2002).

In other instances, the board of regents has become involved in matters that were normally considered in the purview of the shared governance structure, without consultation with the faculty (Scott, 1996). Nonetheless, the board can also provide important support to diversity initiatives because it may have the opportunity and authority to periodically review key measurements in the progress toward achieving diversity.

Administration

The central locus of power on university campuses is the president and executive cabinet comprising the provost or chief academic officer and the vice presidents. Occasionally, the diversity or affirmative action officer serves on the cabinet. The president, as the chief executive, provides the essential leadership for the diversity strategy as articulated in the university's mission and goals. Yet as the campus leader who sets the tone for the campus climate, presidents may often be removed from direct observation of subtle internal barriers.

A survey of 2,594 college presidents by the American Council on Education in 2001 found that despite slight gains in the number of women and minority presidents, the typical college president is a white, Protestant male with an average age of 57.5 years who serves an average of 6.9 years (Basinger, 2002). Although many presidents exhibit extraordinary commitment to diversity, the time needed to transmit this commitment throughout the campus remains a challenge. For this reason, the university president may not be present for the type of long-term transformation required to build and transform a campus.

As academic and administrative leaders, deans are an integral part of the university hierarchy in their oversight of colleges and schools. In providing leadership to departments, deans play an important role in policy setting and ensuring equity in the higher education workplace.

Administrative department heads are also key participants in the management structure. Like academic department heads, administrative department heads can serve as change agents in the workplace. Yet unlike tenured department chairs and faculty, most management employees serve "at will," typically without guarantees of continued employment or the same due process rights as employees with so-called "property rights" to their positions. Given the more tenuous and precarious nature of management employment, even greater reliance must be placed on the management employee's relationship with his or her supervisor and organizational leadership. Administrative department heads must transmit the vision and goals of the leadership throughout the organization. As line managers, they have the ability to influence certain administrative processes of the educational institution. In their responsibility for policy implementation, they directly affect the quality of the work environment for the individuals who report to them.

Unions

The presence of unions for faculty, staff, and graduate teaching assistants on research university campuses can affect the balance of power in the workplace. As of fall 1998, 22 percent of full-time faculty in public research universities were represented by collective bargaining organizations (Bradburn, Skora, and Zimbler, 2002). Faculty unionization has permitted faculty members involved in academic governance to have input into economic issues from an institutionwide perspective (Ehrenberg, Klaff, Kezsbom, and Nagowski, 2004). Faculty unions such as the American Association of University Professors have advanced issues of equity in pay for female faculty members and explored other issues of equity. The issue of diversity has received considerably less recognition and attention from staff unions, perhaps because of the need to focus on a living wage and other fundamental issues (Ehrenberg, Klaff, Kezsbom, and Nagowski, 2004).

As a source of power on campus, union leaders often have influence, visibility, and some degree of access to campus leaders. New models may need to be explored that would enhance partnerships between union and management in building a diverse workplace.

Multicultural Constituencies

Multicultural constituencies on campus serve at the grassroots level to support and articulate issues relating to the participation of minority groups and women. The potential power of these groups lies in their ability to speak in a unified voice and to provide aid and support to individual causes affecting minorities and women. Working from outside the power structure, their influence can be brought to bear on administrative decision making, often through the use of media such as the campus newspaper.

The Power of the Accreditation Model

Just as affirmative action, despite its controversial nature, has fostered changes in the hiring process through an external legal mandate, the diversity criteria of accreditation bodies such as the Middle States Commission on Higher Education, the North Central Association of Colleges and Schools, and the Western Association of Schools and Colleges have provided significant impetus to examine progress in attaining diversity. Yet although diversity criteria are accepted today as part of the accreditation process, the introduction of these criteria on college campuses was initially highly controversial.

When the Middle States agency adopted new guidelines for diversity in 1988, faculty members and college administrators expressed strong concerns that the articulation of a "diversity standard" was intrusive. They charged that diversity criteria would hurt academic quality, encourage quotas, limit campus autonomy and freedom, and affect religious freedom. The outcry against

Middle States resulted in lobbying the U.S. Department of Education to cut off recognition to the accrediting agency.

The specific instance that generated the controversy was the agency's accreditation review of Baruch College of the City University of New York and Westminster Theological Seminary. Middle States indicated that Baruch's percentage of minority faculty was too low (18 percent) and deferred reaccreditation of Baruch mostly for that reason. This action contributed to the resignation of Baruch's president. In the case of Westminster, Middle States threatened to withhold accreditation because of the seminary's resistance to including a woman on its governing board, based on its Calvinist theology (Martin, 1994).

In response, Secretary of Education Lamar Alexander delayed an extension of the agency's recognition, pending a review of its diversity criteria. Many campus presidents, however, wrote in support of the value of diversity criteria. President William J. Maxwell of Jersey City State College wrote, for example, "The multicultural nature of our society is one of its great strengths, and colleges and universities, whether public or independent, have a responsibility to prepare their students for life in the real America of the year 2000" (Jaschik, 1991, p. A18).

Under pressure from the Department of Education, Middle States issued a clarification telling its member institutions that although diversity was encouraged, universities and colleges would not be penalized for failing to meet the guidelines (Leatherman, 1991). On the advice of a federal advisory panel, the department recommended recognition of Middle States for four years. The report issued by the Department of Education recommended that Middle States file an annual report that discussed all recommendations related to diversity issues (Jaschik, 1992).

Despite the controversy generated around the introduction of diversity criteria, external review of progress in diversity recruitment is generally accepted today as part of the periodic assessment process.

Diversity and Decentralization

Institutionwide efforts to counteract and address the ten organizational barriers described in this chapter must take into account the multifaceted nature of the power structure described in the sections above and how power is operationalized in the decentralized subcultures of departments, schools, and administrative entities. Power in higher education enables the continued existence of discrimination through the legitimizing medium of policies and practices (Lindsay, 1994). The department is the microcosm in which organizational policies and informal practices are shaped, interpreted, and applied. Without institutional oversight, the potential for significant disparities may exist. Multiple barriers may exist for the individual minority or female employee, heightening the sense of marginality and exclusion. Most important, these organizational barriers obstruct career progress and success.

The experiences of minority and women faculty differ substantially from those of minority and women administrators in terms of employment status and protections, roles and responsibilities, career development, supervisory and collegial relationships, and professional expectations. In contrast with faculty diversity, few frameworks exist that can assist universities with issues of administrative diversity (Jackson, 2006). In the journey toward understanding how the model of reciprocal empowerment can be implemented in the higher education workplace, the next chapter explores the documented experiences and specific challenges faced by women and minority tenure-track faculty in the academy.

Navigating the Straits: Overcoming Challenges to Faculty Diversity

There is no doubt that, at this point in time, women and minorities must learn to survive the academy as it is. Individual survival is critical; nonetheless, individual survival is a short-sighted goal. We must work toward an academic culture that is committed to the mutual growth and development of all its participants.
                        —Johnsrud and Des Jarlais, 1994, p. 351

A GROWING AND RATHER EXTENSIVE BODY of literature now exists about barriers to diversity in the tenure-track faculty career path, in part because of the research focus of academicians who are engaged in issues related to diversity. With the findings and observations advanced through this research, women faculty have been in the forefront in terms of identification of career-related diversity issues and strategies (see, for example, Cooper and Stevens, 2002b; Glazer-Raymo, 1999; Nidiffer and Bashaw, 2001). Given the significant body of existing research, this chapter focuses on several areas that provide the opportunity to explore the themes of the monograph in greater specificity: faculty hiring, tenure progression, and rewards and recognition for contributions to diversity.

A number of factors differentiate the tenure-track faculty career path from that of upper-level administrators in research universities: (1) the relatively homogenous path of advancement; (2) the localized nature of departmental politics and the formal and informal impact of departmental decision making on tenure progression; (3) the peer-to-peer relationships involved in faculty success; (4) the presence of some procedural protections in faculty tenure processes; (5) the expectation for independent scholarship, research, and publication in addition to teaching and service; and (6) the pivotal nature of the tenure decision as the gateway to permanent employment after a relatively long (usually six-year) preparatory period in the university environment.

Consistent with the themes of this monograph, a broadened view has emerged in recent literature on faculty diversity that specifically recognizes the importance of grounding the framework for understanding faculty careers in contemporary psychological and sociological theory (Blackburn and Lawrence, 1995). From this perspective, faculty work performance, motivation, and productivity are affected by the interaction of the faculty member with the institution in terms not only of the culture and climate of the academic environment but also of the individual faculty member's sociodemographic background, career history, self-knowledge, and social understanding (Blackburn and Lawrence, 1995). Because cultural, structural, and behavioral elements are dynamic, interrelated components of the higher education workplace (Ragins, 1995), the complex interplay of behavioral and organizational elements in the workplace can affect the ability of women and minority faculty to surmount specific challenges in the faculty career progression.

As the point of entry to an academic institution, hiring processes represent the nexus or intersection between departmental culture and decision-making processes. The next section reviews issues related to faculty hiring with a view to identifying strategies to address patterns of underrepresentation in public research universities.

Faculty Hiring for Diversity: Defeating the Narrowing Sieve

The metaphor of the narrowing sieve can be applied to the screening process that occurs during faculty hiring. To slip through the bands of the sieve, the candidate must convince the members of the departmental hiring committee that she or he fits in with the dominant norms and culture. Moore (1987) points out the difficulty of hiring black faculty on white campuses and the prevalence of myths about lowering departmental standards, needing extra resources, not pressuring the search committee to hire minorities, and having an insufficient pool of minority candidates. Once the minority candidate is interviewed, the candidate is unlikely to have advocates on the search committee or be a recipient of the "old boy" system of academic patronage (Moore, 1987).

In a study of 689 faculty searches undertaken between 1995 and 1998 at three large elite public research universities, researchers found that successful hires of underrepresented faculty were most likely to occur when the job description was linked to diversity (either through the program, subfield, or job qualifications related to diversity) and when institutional programs of intervention (search waiver, spousal hire, targeted hires, incentive funds) were involved (Smith, Turner, Osei-Kofi, and Richards, 2004). In this study, only 5 percent of hires resulted in the choice of an underrepresented faculty member when these conditions were not present, and even when diversity indicators or special hiring situations were involved, 65 percent of those hired were white (Smith, Turner, Osei-Kofi, and Richards, 2004).

Frequently, the "pipeline defense" or lack of new Ph.D. graduates is cited as the reason minority and female scholars are not hired for tenure-track positions. Yet this defense ignores the fact that minority and women scholars can be recruited from tenure and non-tenure-track positions, including postdoctoral positions at other institutions (White, 2005). Moreover, a study of four hundred scholars who had recently completed their doctoral degrees with fellowships from the Ford, Spencer, and Mellon Foundations reveals that the myth of bidding wars for minorities is unfounded (Smith, 1995). More than half of the scientists from minority backgrounds in the study were not offered faculty positions, and many were holding their third or fourth postdoctoral position (Smith, 1995). Only 11 percent of the scholars from underrepresented groups received more than one job offer, 20 percent took postdoctoral positions, 10 percent were underemployed, and 14 percent took the only position they were offered (Smith, 1995).

Rather than telescoping inward, hiring processes can present a more expansive view of the disciplinary needs of a department, its teaching goals, and its research endeavors. The diversity of the search committee is an important factor in the recruitment of women and minorities to faculty ranks. Virginia Polytechnic Institute and State University, for example, requires a minority or woman on each faculty search committee. A study of faculty search committees at Virginia Tech found that women have different points of view from their male counterparts (Schwindt, Hall, and Davis, 1998).

Another important area in the search process involves the way faculty candidates are interviewed off campus at major conferences. These preinterviews are essentially screening interviews and may not be conducted in the same structured fashion or with the same rigor as on-campus interviews. Records may not be kept of the results or how candidates are screened.

How an advertisement is written can narrow the field of applicants to a particular subdiscipline and unnecessarily limit the possibility for a broader range of applicants. Once the position has been advertised, clear criteria for the screening process that are closely related to the position description need to be developed to ensure consistency and relevancy to stated job requirements.

Best practices in minority faculty hiring include Kent State University in Kent, Ohio, the University of Kansas, in Lawrence, and the University of Wisconsin at Madison.

At Kent State University, an expansive list of suggestions prepared by the Office of the Provost and Vice Provost for Diversity and Academic Initiatives recommends consideration of minority directories such as the *Minority and Women's Doctoral Directory,* looking beyond traditional age groups and traditional recruiting sources, and fostering a pipeline for candidates. Recruitment is viewed as a continuous process that can benefit from contacts by administrators and faculty members at professional conferences and at other gatherings to identify and actively search for diverse candidates of interest. Bridge funds are available for minority appointments until departments can assume these costs ("Implementing Hiring for Diversity," n.d.).

At the University of Kansas, the Blueprint Committee has developed "Minority Faculty Recruitment Resources and Guidelines" that identify strategies for increasing minority representation, including scholars-in-residence programs, interinstitutional exchanges, bridge funds, and short-term appointments for faculty from historically black colleges and universities. Each search committee must be certified in equal opportunity and affirmative action training ("Minority Faculty Recruitment," 2006).

The University of Wisconsin at Madison has established a strategic hiring initiative that devotes $1 million per year to fund initial years of high-priority faculty hires. Dual-career funding and postdoctoral fellowships are also available ("Faculty Strategic Hiring Initiative," 2006).

Other strategies to increase faculty diversity include hiring women and minorities who have completed all but the dissertation for their doctoral degrees and then assisting them through faculty development programs, creating financial incentives such as "two-for-one" programs that allow a department to fill an additional line when a minority candidate is hired, and supporting internal candidates such as promising doctoral students (Tack and Patitu, 1992). The tendency of some departments and disciplines represented in the sixty-two research universities of the Association of American Universities to select degree holders from AAU institutions for teaching positions may limit opportunities to seek and hire diverse candidates from historically black universities and other institutions.

The following section discusses the hurdles of the tenure process with reference to the particular challenges faced by minority and women faculty. These challenges may be exacerbated by a number of factors in the psychosocial environment of the department and institution.

Whitewater Rafting: The Tenure Journey

In the tenure decision, the interplay of structural, behavioral, and cultural factors coalesce in a single administrative action. From this perspective, the tenure decision can be described as a complex rite of passage (Tierney and Rhoads, 1994) that involves locally determined, merit-driven assessments of accomplishments (McDonough, 2002). To be successful in this rite of passage, pretenure faculty must pay careful attention to institutional culture from the start, take control as the engineer on the tenure journey, and address the journey in planned and systematic ways (Bronstein and Ramaley, 2002).

Role of the Department Chair in the Tenure Process

As noted earlier, the department is the cultural environment that determines how minority and women faculty are welcomed and supported, how conflicts are addressed and resolved, and how power is shared. Unlike administrators and staff, faculty function in an environment of peers, although the department chair provides a lead administrative role. The department chair not only sets the tone in the department but also holds a key tenure vote and a decisive leadership role on departmental personnel committees. As an established link to administration, the department chair can, through years in the institution, hold considerable credibility and influence. Yet as a study of two hundred ninety faculty in a large public university reveals, despite influence in administrative areas, the chair is often regarded as having little informal influence in the areas of research and teaching (DeVries, 1975).

By adopting a language of encouragement, chairs and faculty colleagues can communicate that the presence of minority faculty is not simply a response to a federal mandate and does not represent the lowering of academic standards (Chandler, 1993). The influence of departmental colleagues and the chair begins with the job interview and the interviewee's introduction to the culture of the department. After hiring, the departmental culture is expressed during the pretenure period through the presence or absence of mentoring, support, advocacy, and other enabling conditions (McDonough, 2002).

Departmental Climate and Influence on Personnel Processes

Because the "sacred grove" of the academy has been limited until recently to white males, the entry of women and minorities may be perceived as threatening the traditional occupants as a result of the potential for change in values and activities (Cooper and Stevens, 2002b). Because the membership of personnel committees evaluating faculty for tenure is often predominantly male and majority, women and minorities may not have attained the critical mass necessary to make a difference in the tenure review processes of junior faculty. Without such critical mass, the presence of women and minorities in small numbers can instead result in increased visibility, heightened scrutiny, differential standards, and pressures to conform (Bronstein and Farnsworth, 1998).

Collegiality and fitting in are essential aspects of gaining entrance to the tenured sacred grove. Women and minorities who experience the pressure to fit in must engage in "smile work"—a culturally driven strategy to present oneself as pleasing and agreeable to fit in (Tierney and Bensimon, 1996). Behaving like a good colleague and a team player may create pressures for women and minorities to falsify or disguise their identities and to be more accommodating and sometimes even submissive. This pressure leads to feelings of powerlessness and loss of self and self-confidence (Tierney and Bensimon, 1996).

The poignant experiences of Curry (2002) as an African American faculty member facing the hurdles of promotion and tenure validate this cultural pressure and demonstrate the fact that the academy is not a disconnected structure but mirrors the predominant American identity as both "imperious and institutionalized" (p. 118). In this sense, the academy "defines who and what is valued and the ways in which aspects of an individual's identity are to be treated" (Curry, 2002, p. 118). The mutually reinforcing phenomena of discrimination and physical identifiability (Aguirre and Turner, 1998) take shape in forms of behavior that include the need to view the successful minority faculty member as an exception. Yet as Curry explains, "To perceive of oneself as an exception, different, unique, extraordinary, is the beginning of one's participation in the process of coaptation. It is to suffer a loss of identity. It is a high price to pay for belonging. For the novice or pioneer, survival in the academy has taken the form of disintegration of the self" (p. 119).

Further evidence of the impact of climate on tenure success is provided in a study of five hundred sixty faculty at a major research university undertaken in 1991 (Bronstein and Farnsworth, 1998). Women faculty were 67 percent more likely than men faculty to have experienced disparaging remarks or reactions to their work or potential, including undervaluing their credentials or questioning their qualifications (Bronstein and Farnsworth, 1998). In addition, women in tenure-track positions were more than four times as likely as men to report inappropriate reference to some personal aspect of their lives in their work experiences and twice as likely to have experienced at least one attempt to undermine fair process (Bronstein and Farnsworth, 1998). In fact, these forms of behavioral discrimination have been shown to undermine the professional confidence of women faculty, diminish their sense of belonging, and create uncertainty relative to success in tenure processes (Blakemore, Switzer, DiIorio, and Fairchild, 1997; Bronstein and Farnsworth, 1998).

A recent study undertaken at six research universities found that junior minority faculty reported more pressure to conform to departmental colleagues in their political views than white colleagues, were less satisfied with the influence they had over their research focus, and were less likely than white colleagues to report that tenure decisions were based on performance rather than relationships, demographic background, or politics (Trower and Bleak, 2004).

Viewed as a continuum, the road toward tenure has critical "turning points" that can occur very quickly (Boice, 1993). A study of eighty-four new and midcareer faculty that included both women and minorities demonstrates that these turning points come early, may be replicated even at midcareer, occur with surprising and even devastating speed, and appear to be irreversible (Boice, 1993). Several behavioral indicators characterize these turning points— feeling isolated from colleagues, a sense of collegial disapproval, internalized self-doubt relative to competence, and ultimately a resultant sense of victimization and suspicion (Boice, 1993). These behavioral indicators were accompanied by greater stress among women and minority faculty compared with their white male counterparts (Boice, 1993).

As the discussion of mentoring in the previous chapter has shown, an important strategy for untenured faculty members to cope with a potential lack of support in the department is to locate allies outside the department and to build networks and alliances. The difficulty minority group members have in obtaining both social and instrumental workplace support has emerged as a central theme in the organizational literature (Ibarra, 1995). Having a sponsor—senior minority and women faculty who will help untenured minority and female faculty find entrance to political networks and advance their position in the tenure process—is critical (Aguirre and Martinez, 1993). Building alliances on campus through committee and service work and through relationships with influential faculty and administrators can help counteract negative influences in the department.

The powerful impact of a lack of sponsorship, differing standards, and stereotypes in the faculty evaluation process is described in the first-hand account of Professor Yolanda Flores Niemann (1999). As a Mexican American doctoral student, Niemann was hired without a search by the university where she had just completed her doctoral studies. The circumstances of her hiring created active animosity among some of the department faculty. Her journal reveals how the stigma of incompetence associated with the affirmative action label gradually eroded her self-confidence and exacerbated her vulnerability (Niemann, 1999).

Saddled with an unprecedented teaching and advising load, Niemann handled both graduate and undergraduate seminars and thesis advisement. Her third-year review was overlooked and then administered atypically. Despite the fact she had unusually high ratings in her teaching evaluations, she was challenged directly in her third-year review on the only two negative evaluations in the stack of reviews. She was further advised to disassociate herself from any ethnic- or culture-related research or reviews. The effects of stigmatization had psychological, physical, and professional effects on her. With a shattered sense of self-confidence, Niemann sought another position at a different university, restored her focus, and published a dozen articles in two years. She was convinced that had she stayed at the first institution, her identity might not be recovered (Niemann, 1999). This documented experience reveals the damaging effect of lack of mentoring and workplace support on pretenure faculty.

Institutional initiatives that provide support to women and minority pretenure faculty such as Niemann include attention to clarification of tenure and promotion criteria, explicit definition of expectations in letters of appointment, and the delivery of thorough and constructive feedback through timely performance evaluations (Johnsrud and Des Jarlais, 1994). Formalized personnel procedures that address evaluative criteria can limit the extraordinary scrutiny of female and minority faculty (Kulis, 1997). Institutionally sponsored networking activities can include efforts to provide funds for cross-disciplinary research in areas of interest to minority and women faculty (Turner, 2002). Professional development programs designed to address the issues of multiple marginality can assist pretenure faculty in the classroom and during administrative review (Turner, 2002). University administrators need to identify trends in academic departments where newly hired women and minorities have not been successful and address these patterns. Departments may attempt to individualize each problem, obscuring the fact that women and minorities have encountered similar obstacles in the same department over time ("Tenure in a Chilly Climate," 1999). Building awareness of behavioral barriers and how oppression occurs through thousands of small interactions rather than in big incidents is also critical ("Tenure in a Chilly Climate," 1999).

Tenure Denial and Discrimination Claims

Relatively few tenure denial cases filed under discrimination statutes have been successful based on the actual merits of the academic decision. Most successful cases have been based on procedural issues rather than on substantive determinations. Although in some instances courts have viewed favorably the evaluations of peer review committees and external reviewers in reaching decisions, they have been generally unwilling to function as "super tenure review committees" (Leap, 1995, p. 8). This reluctance to enter the arena of tenure decisions is because of the relation of tenure to academic freedom and deference to academic judgment. As a result, when peer review committees and other external reviewers support tenure recommendations, the courts have given weight to these evaluative judgments in tenure denial cases such as *Kunda* v. *Muhlenberg College* (621 F.2d 532 [3rd Cir. 1980]) (Baez, 2002).

The concept of academic freedom emerged from the autocratic atmosphere of nineteenth-century Germany for both faculty and students as *Lernfreiheit* (freedom of learning) and *Lehrfreiheit* (freedom of teaching) (Kramer, 1982, cited in Leap, 1995). In the United States, an incident that occurred in 1900 when Mrs. Leland Stanford, the sole trustee of Stanford University, demanded that Professor Edward Ross be fired for his inflammatory and negative comments related to Asian immigration laid the groundwork for the concept of academic freedom and the tenure structure (Tierney, 2002). Academic freedom is based on the need to protect the rights of faculty members to teach, publish, and do research without fear of retribution or sanction.

A study of fifty-two cases filed by tenure-track faculty who were denied tenure or reappointment and alleged discrimination based on racial or national origin reveals that faculty won only 31 percent or sixteen cases (Baez, 2002). These cases also reveal a troubling pattern. Of the cases filed against black institutions, 50 percent of the cases were successful (four of eight cases), and all won on substantive grounds. By contrast, white institutions were successful in more than 70 percent of their cases, with only two losses on substantive grounds (Baez, 2002). Scholars have suggested that claims of racial discrimination are extremely difficult to prove except in cases when the faculty member is white and the institution is historically black, a trend that places a heavier legal burden of proof on historically black institutions (Baez and Centra, 1995).

Claims filed using Title VII as a basis can be filed in two areas: disparate treatment and disparate impact. Disparate treatment claims allege differential treatment of the individual based on a protected characteristic, whereas disparate impact claims allege discrimination against a certain class of people based on protected characteristics. Both types of claims are difficult to win because intentional individual acts that show concrete examples of malice or discriminatory intent must be proved for claims of disparate treatment, and systemic patterns of discrimination that affect protected groups disproportionately must be shown in disparate impact cases (Baez, 2002; Leap, 1995). Comparative data among candidates for tenure is often difficult to establish because of the application of qualitative and sometimes subjective criteria (Leap, 1995).

A pivotal Supreme Court decision in *University of Pennsylvania* v. *EEOC* (493 U.S. 182 [1990]) set the stage for allowing access to confidential tenure review files. In this case, Professor Rosalie Tung, an Asian American associate professor at the University of Pennsylvania's Wharton School of Business, alleged that following her rejection of the chair's sexual advances, the chair retaliated by filing negative letters with the personnel committee despite her record of research that was comparable with that of other faculty members (Glazer-Raymo, 1999). At that time, only one tenured woman faculty member was in the department and in the entire business school of more than three hundred faculty. After refusing requests by the EEOC for access to peer review documents, the university appealed to the Supreme Court, which ruled unanimously that First Amendment coverage of academic privilege did not protect the tenure review files and that access to confidential tenure review files is relevant in cases of employment discrimination (Glazer-Raymo, 1999). The U.S. District Court rendered a similar finding in *Weinstock* v. *Columbia University* (1996, No. 95, Civ. 0569), asserting the necessity of investigating the peer review material itself to determine whether evaluative decisions in the tenure process were discriminatory (Glazer-Raymo, 1999).

In this regard, Nakanishi (1996) points out that "redacted" tenure summaries that eliminate information as well as the names and signatures of reviewers used in his own tenure review case at the University of California at Los Angeles precluded full examination of evaluative materials. This information was subsequently revealed only through the testimony of a dozen faculty members in grievance hearings. He further cites the common misconception that Asian Pacific Americans do not face discriminatory employment practices in higher education and will walk away from unfair tenure and denial decisions without protest (Nakanishi, 1996).

The legal arena has drawn attention to the importance of accountability in the application of standards and criteria in the tenure process through access to tenure records when discrimination is alleged. The increasing unionization of faculty, particularly in public institutions, has also resulted in an increase in procedural protections in the tenure process. These forms of due process may include, for example, requirements for stating the reasons for tenure denial, notification periods in advance of nonrenewal, and avenues of appeal or reconsideration.

The next section examines the potential for developing evaluation and reward programs and structures that recognize contributions to diversity. Such programs not only call attention to the value of diversity but also assist in the process of institutional transformation.

Reward Structures, Intentionality, and Diversity

Although the importance of diversity in hiring, retention, and promotion decisions has been widely acknowledged, the notion of rewarding diversity in faculty evaluative processes has received significantly less attention and even remains somewhat controversial. Yet without modification of the criteria by which faculty are recognized and rewarded, faculty focus and activities will remain unchanged (Diamond, 1993). Because institutional support is conveyed through formal recognition of activities consistent with institutional values, recognition for faculty diversity work will ensure the continuation of such contributions (Olsen, Maple, and Stage, 1995).

Further, when universities provide recognition for contributions to faculty diversity, this recognition can serve as a catalyst for cultural change. To achieve a coherent program for supporting and recognizing diversity requires intentionality in diversity planning so that the sum total of the institution's processes, resource decisions, infrastructure, and culture advances the institution's commitment to diversity (Lima, 2003).

A clearly articulated institutional mission statement referencing diversity is the starting point for this correlative process. Explicit identification of the importance of diversity in the institution's mission statement begins to build faculty morale around the issue of diversity, as the college's or university's mission and goals are the key to the values of the culture communicated through campus ceremonies and symbols (Austin, Rice, and Splete, 1991, cited in Diamond, 1993). In this regard, a study of faculty at four historically black colleges and universities reveals that faculty found articulation of clear institutional values positive and helpful to them in the socialization process (Johnson and Harvey, 2002).

Recognition for diversity work can also take shape through a broadened definition of scholarship. A structure that assesses and rewards faculty achievements in terms of this new paradigm is the American Council on Education (2005). Other initiatives that support success in formal tenure processes include developing incentives for mentoring colleagues, establishing local guidelines at the departmental or school level to interpret tenure criteria, and training evaluators in nondiscriminatory application of tenure guidelines (American Council on Education, 2005). Promotion and tenure committees need to reflect a commitment to diversity and interdisciplinary, or collaborative research needs to be valued as much as independent research in the tenure process (Trower and Chait, 2002).

A complex set of questions arises in terms of how diversity contributions might be recognized in service activities. Based on their own experiences of marginalization, minority faculty may be more likely to have community service as a personal goal, assume personal responsibility for social change, and place higher importance on moral, affective, and civic development of students (Antonio, 2002). Yet a clear danger of further isolation arises when only minority faculty are engaged in service related to diversity. The demands for minority faculty to serve on committees related to minority issues can in fact make these faculty peripheral participants and prevent them from participating in mainstream decision making (Aguirre and Martinez, 1993).

In support of this perspective, another study reports that eleven women and minority faculty felt that they were not highly regarded because of their involvement in multicultural or feminist issues (Bronstein, 1993). In addition, when minority faculty are "showcased" on committees or commissions, they may engage in self-questioning when they see that they are "being called on to represent their ethnicity, not their professional competence" (Johnsrud and Sadao, 1998, p. 335). The dilemma of being strangers rather than competitors in an institution's mainstream activities creates difficulty for minority faculty who wish to encourage the success of minority students (Aguirre and Martinez, 1993).

Research has shown that women and minorities may place greater priority on advising students because of the special sense of responsibility to students from similar demographic backgrounds. In addition, women and minorities may place greater emphasis on curricular and pedagogical issues because of their perceived need to correct biases in traditional curricular approaches (Park, 1996). Because an inverse relationship has been demonstrated between teaching and faculty pay and high positive correlations exist between research productivity and pay in most universities (Fairweather, 1996), minority faculty who emphasize service, advising, and teaching may not be recognized for these activities in terms of compensation. Further, given the importance of publication and research in attaining tenure, focus on service and teaching activities can even detract from progress toward tenure. As a result, recognition of the importance of the scholarships of application, integration, and teaching identified in Boyer's *Scholarship Reconsidered: Priorities of the Professoriate* (1990) is critical.

Despite the challenges posed by incorporating recognition for diversity into faculty processes, specific identification of faculty contributions to diversity in departmental leadership, curricular efforts, service, and research is an important lever in the transformation of departmental and institutional climate. Moving from the vantage point of recognizing individual faculty contributions, the next chapter examines institutionwide approaches to diversity assessment and planning.

Best Practices in Diversity Planning and Assessment

This struggle may be a moral one, or it may be a physical one, and it may be both moral and physical, but it must be a struggle. Power concedes nothing without a demand. It never did and it never will. Find out just what any people will quietly submit to and you have found out the exact measure of injustice and wrong [that] will be imposed on them, and these will continue till they are resisted with either words or blows, or with both.

—Frederick Douglass
The Frederick Douglass Papers, 1857, para. 5

THE INSIGHTS OF ABOLITIONIST FREDERICK DOUGLASS illuminate the difficulty of achieving the model of reciprocal empowerment in the workplace. In the context of higher education, institutional programs and policies that create the potential for shared power, collaboration, and true partnership for women, minority faculty, and administrators are best practices that transcend mere structural diversity and enable inclusion at the core of the administrative and academic enterprise. These practices *empower* diverse faculty and staff to be successful through mentoring, participation in decision making, leadership and career development, and opportunities for promotion.

This chapter reviews emerging models in diversity planning and assessment with a specific focus on how these models can be and are being implemented in public research universities. Because affirmative action has barely changed higher education's workplace demographics and has achieved much greater success in

---

the hiring and advancement of white female faculty and staff, the attainment of structural diversity for ethnic and racial minorities remains an issue. Yet in addressing retention and inclusion as institutions achieve more advanced stages of diversity, concrete programs that foster the empowerment of minorities and women are urgently needed. As Frederick Douglass's words indicate, without participation and inclusion, minority and women faculty and staff will remain strangers, isolated and without institutional support. The report of the Kerner Commission (1968), developed under the leadership of President Lyndon Johnson, points out that there are two societies in America: one white and one black, still separate and unequal. From a twenty-first-century vantage point, institutional intervention is needed to overcome the vestiges of this social divide and to ensure that women and minority faculty and administrators are not marginalized but truly included and empowered.

An extensive review of contemporary programs and practices in faculty and staff diversity suggests that many diversity strategies essentially deal only with affirmative action and hiring and do not move beyond the point of hiring to retention and reciprocal empowerment through coaching, mentoring, professional growth, and institutional sponsorship. As a result and in the absence of a more comprehensive approach, the organizational and behavioral barriers identified in this monograph will remain unaddressed. Even seemingly "neutral" administrative practices that do not promote or actualize the goals of reciprocal empowerment may actually serve to perpetuate existing barriers for faculty and staff.

One of the few national education and mentoring programs that expressly addresses the idea of advancement into positions of power in higher education is the American Council on Education's Fellows Program. This program has fostered the professional development of talented and diverse faculty and administrators by providing fellows the opportunity to work on a different campus with presidents and senior leaders for an extended period of time.

A promising development over the past decade is the emergence of a new instrument in higher education—the diversity strategic plan. As noted earlier, the majority of these plans have been created at large public universities and community colleges (see the appendix). This finding is consistent with the 1989 American Council on Education survey of 456 colleges and universities, which reported the greatest levels of programmatic activity to increase minority participation at doctoral institutions (Hurtado, 1996). The importance of federal funding and the related requirement for affirmative action compliance may indeed be a factor in this level of activity (Konrad and Pfeffer, 1996). And the greater availability of resources to address these issues at public doctoral universities may also play a role.

Diversity strategic plans are a preeminent best practice because they draw attention to the importance of diversity and establish measurable goals, taking diversity off the back burner for the whole campus to see. Without concrete goals and objectives, the work of diversity becomes amorphous and ambiguous. A diversity strategic plan communicates the importance of diversity to both external and internal constituencies and helps ensure that diversity has a place in institutional resource allocation and prioritization. These processes in turn strengthen institutional accountability (Smith and Wolf-Wendel, 2005).

The Twenty-First-Century Diversity Strategic Plan

The twenty-first-century diversity strategic plan is an instrument that synthesizes the findings of diversity evaluation, incorporates analysis of gaps between the current and desired state of diversity, and situates the goals for diversity in the larger context of the institution's strategic agenda. These plans have been spearheaded by institutional leaders who not only articulate the vision of diversity but also recognize the importance of the infrastructure and resources needed to achieve a culture of diversity. Diversity strategic plans are linked to an institution's overall strategic plan. To be successful, it cannot be an isolated or separate effort or appended as an afterthought to strategic planning.

A diversity strategic plan is instead a forward-looking instrument that emphasizes both internal and external engagement between and among communities of interest. In light of its value as a communication tool, a diversity strategic plan is an instrument of persuasion and a vehicle of change. It demonstrates the business case for diversity, typically through its vision statement written by the chancellor, president, or chief diversity officer. This motivating vision is frequently described as an important element in the change process (Eckel and Kezar, 2003; Humphreys, 2000).

If diversity plans focus narrowly on structural diversity, the broader questions related to systemic cultural transformation, changes in campus administrative practices, progress toward student learning goals, or the enhancement of intellectual diversity will not be addressed (Humphreys, 2000). Although specific approaches may vary based on institutional characteristics, strategic diversity plans typically include a number of key elements:

1. *A values, vision, or mission statement* that identifies the importance and value of diversity and inclusion and establishes links to strategic institutional goals in a broader regional, national, and global context;
2. *A conceptual framework* that provides the overarching rationale for diversity and articulates the areas of focus or dimensions for study;
3. *Input* from campus constituencies, diversity councils or commissions, and governance councils in plan development;
4. *Objectives* and milestones presented in a multiyear format;
5. *Accountability* for fulfillment of goals for departments, divisions, and executive positions or the collaboration needed to achieve objectives;
6. *Incentives* and recognition for hiring or other diversity-related initiatives;
7. *Assessment mechanisms* such as campus climate surveys or other diversity assessment tools to monitor progress and provide data;
8. *Infrastructure, budgetary, and staffing resources* necessary to implement the plan.

An overview of representative diversity strategic plans in public research universities is provided in the appendix. Examples of diversity strategic plans with concrete objectives related to the realization of reciprocal empowerment in the workplace originate in several universities:

The University of Arizona's diversity action plan (2003) has clear components relating to empowerment. It addresses the issue of correcting salary inequities for faculty and staff from underrepresented groups through initiation of campuswide compensation studies and the identification of funds to address those inequities. In addition, the plan emphasizes the need to review faculty teaching and service responsibilities annually and to clarify criteria for promotion. Of particular interest is the statement that evaluations of subtle discriminatory behavior should be included in both informal feedback and annual administrative reviews.

Auburn University's strategic diversity plan (2005) includes the development of a communication plan for diversity, career development and succession planning programs for leadership development, mandatory diversity training for supervisors, and mentoring programs for faculty and staff. The strategic diversity plan also calls for incorporation of diversity as a performance dimension in annual appraisals for faculty, administrators, professionals, and university staff. Specific outcomes of the plan include the establishment of a recruitment fund for faculty and administrators, an African American faculty outreach fund, and a professional development funding program for tenure-track African American faculty members (Auburn University, 2005).

Virginia Polytechnic and State University in Blacksburg, Virginia, has a highly comprehensive diversity plan that includes the goal of developing and institutionalizing a system of responsibility, accountability, and recognition for campus diversity. The plan identifies the need for a task force to review diversity and multicultural aspects of faculty roles and rewards ("Faces of Change," 2000). Results of the plan include the formation of the Commission on Equal Opportunity and Diversity with the authority to recommend university policy on diversity; the Diversity Research Initiative Fund for faculty, staff, and students; and the Diversity Awards Program for faculty, staff, and students.

The University of Washington in Seattle developed its own diversity appraisal program, which requested a series of reports from three campuses and 150 departments describing diversity efforts in seven areas, including staff, faculty, and campus climate. Based on these reports, the diversity appraisal steering committee issued a set of priority recommendations. A two-year budget was allocated to fund projects addressing the recommendations in the report, among them the need for diversity-related objectives above and beyond federally mandated affirmative action goals and the creation of formal leadership and mentoring programs to provide pathways into administration for underrepresented faculty and staff (University of Washington, 2004).

A Conceptual Approach to Diversity Assessment

As the diversity strategic plan sets the stage and the parameters for change, assessment is the vehicle for monitoring whether or not change has occurred and providing impetus in the accomplishment of planned goals or targets. The real value of the assessment of diversity lies in its ability to demonstrate tangible outcomes and to insist on progress.

Recent scholarship on diversity in higher education is of critical value in guiding and structuring how such assessment is conducted (Garcia and others, 2001). To counter the constant attacks on affirmative action, a research-based approach shifts attention to the issues of educational quality and excellence through curricular efforts and attention to climate (Smith and others, 2000). With the Supreme Court's recent endorsement of the importance of diversity on college campuses, research-based models that support broad-based diversity are fully consistent with contemporary legal interpretations.

A new conceptual approach to diversity planning and assessment links organizational learning and diversity (Smith and Parker, 2005). This approach emphasizes development of institutional capacity to sustain change. The organizational learning model focuses on "the process of the effort and takes action to ensure progress toward success by making changes or corrections as necessary" (Smith and Parker, 2005, p. 116). This organic model provides the opportunity for course correction midstream rather than looking backward after projects have been completed. Because organizational learning relates to the institution's core work, assessment draws on institutional data, builds on academic discourse relating to educational outcomes, encourages ownership of the process, and engages cross-institutional decision makers (Smith and Parker, 2005).

To be successful, the diversity assessment model needs to be cross-institutional, multidimensional, and multilevel. Further, it needs to determine the extent to which diversity efforts have permeated the entire institution and the balance between macro- and microdiversity efforts (Knox and Teraguchi, 2005). In this regard, three measures can be used: centrality, pervasiveness, and integration (Knox and Teraguchi, 2005). One of the most cogent examples of a multidimensional, cross-institutional framework is the model developed by Smith (1995) that examines access and success, climate and intergroup relations, education and scholarship, and institutional viability and vitality (cited in Musil and others, 1999). Several research universities have adopted this framework in constructing their diversity strategic plans. Each dimension of the framework generates key indicators for evaluating progress. The indicator of student access and success can be measured, for example, by persistence and retention data relative to race, ethnicity and gender; socioeconomic data; pursuit of advanced degrees; and transfer among fields (Smith and Parker, 2005). Following the approach of determining the extent to which diversity has permeated the organization, each indicator could be examined in terms of pervasiveness, centrality, and integration (Knox and Teraguchi, 2005).

Another viable approach to the assessment of diversity uses accreditation criteria as the framework. The value of this approach is to ensure that diversity planning is an integral part of the accreditation process, avoiding redundancy and duplication in strategic assessment. In particular, the innovative accreditation process developed by the Academic Quality Improvement Project of the Higher Learning Commission of the North Central Association of Colleges and Schools could serve as a systematic diversity assessment model. The program, begun in 1999, is based on the principles of continuous improvement and emphasizes quality and institutional self-awareness. Among its nine assessment criteria are those for valuing people, helping students learn, measuring effectiveness, building collaborative relationships, and leading and communicating (Academic Quality Improvement Project, 2002). As an example, the criterion of valuing people could be used to examine the ways in which the institution values diversity through its talent management strategies as well as the value employees find in affiliation with the institution (Ledford, 2002).

Multilevel diversity assessment not only evaluates structural diversity outcomes but also explores the secondary layers of espoused values and underlying assumptions in the institution's culture (Schein, 1992). Although structural assessment reviews indicators such as hiring and promotion, deeper-level assessment seeks to gauge psychological climate and behavioral barriers. It explores the questions of how minority and female faculty and staff are perceived and how they perceive themselves functioning in the campus environment (Hurtado, 1996). Identifying how minority and women faculty and staff experience the behavioral and psychological elements of the campus climate is challenging in terms of devising instruments that allow for the hidden and subtle aspects of the climate to be recorded in meaningful analysis. Given the hazards of predetermining answers through the types of questions asked, individual narratives, exit interviews, cultural audits, climate studies, and focus groups are important tools for eliciting the first-hand experiences of minority and female faculty and staff.

A sample culture audit asks individuals what major changes they have seen in the organization, what attracted them to the organization, what makes the organization good at what it does, and to what extent their expectations have been fulfilled in the organization. It also asks about unmet expectations and frustrations, what is required to be successful at the organization, and whether individuals consider themselves successful (Thomas, 1991).

The Diversity Scorecard

As a measure of progress in the institutionalization of diversity, the diversity scorecard is an increasingly popular assessment tool that derived from the balanced scorecard developed in the 1990s by Kaplan and Norton to clarify strategy and translate strategy into action (Arveson, 1998). The versatility of the scorecard is that it can be tailored to address different aspects of diversity change initiatives and serve as a tool for generating discussion, identifying gaps, and ensuring progress. The scorecard's popularity in current management literature derives from its ability to crystallize key measurements in an easily intelligible format. The diversity scorecard can be adapted to reflect different conceptual or organizational approaches to assessment. As a measurement tool, it selects concrete objectives derived from the organization's strategy and linked to its diversity goals (Hubbard, 2004; see also Becker, Huselid, and Ulrich, 2001; Huselid, Becker, and Beatty, 2005). The diversity scorecard is a way of turning data analysis into "an intervention tool—a catalyst for change," as "what gets measured is noticed" (Bensimon, 2004, p. 47).

The Inclusive Excellence Scorecard developed by Williams, Berger, and McClendon (2005) is another example of a cross-dimensional and institutionwide scorecard that integrates the four areas of access and equity, diversity in the formal and informal curriculum, climate, and student learning. Levers for change are senior leadership and accountability, vision and buy-in, capacity building, and resources. The Inclusive Excellence Change Model takes into account the organizational dynamics represented by political, bureaucratic, collegial, and symbolic dimensions of the campus culture (Williams, Berger, and McClendon, 2005).

The sample Structural Diversity Scorecard shown in Exhibit 3 reviews human resource employment approaches in terms of four key areas: access, recruitment and retention, proactive human resource processes, and institutional values and receptivity (Chun, 2004).

Exhibit 3
Structural Diversity Scorecard

ACCESS	Yes	No	Score
The institution has developed and disseminated an affirmative action statement.			
An annual affirmative planning process is required of all organizational units.			
The affirmative action plan includes goals and timetables that are updated annually.			
Organizational units are held accountable for reaching affirmative action goals.			
The institution develops and enforces policies against discrimination.			
Discrimination complaint procedures have been widely disseminated.			
Affirmative action advisory groups and facilitators assist with implementation of the affirmative action plan.			
Training is provided on the affirmative action plan.			
Sexual harassment training is provided on a regular basis.			

(continued)

Exhibit 3 (*Continued*)

ACCESS   *Yes No Score*

RECRUITMENT AND RETENTION

Policies and procedures have been developed and
  disseminated regarding how searches are conducted.

The institution records, monitors, and analyzes applicant
  demographic information for protected classes.

Demographic applicant information is compiled and
  compared with prior years on an annual basis.

Proactive search and recruitment strategies are undertaken
  to increase the diversity of applicant pools.

All job advertisements include an institutional affirmative
  action/EEO statement and are written to attract a diverse
  applicant pool.

Screening criteria are clearly defined.

The composition of search committees is monitored to ensure
  diversity among search committee members.

Training on interviewing is provided to search committees
  and hiring authorities.

Affirmative action briefs each search committee on procedures,
  compliance, and goals.

A "pipeline approach" is used to strengthen the advancement
  of protected classes.

PROACTIVE HUMAN RESOURCE PROCESSES

Compensation audits are undertaken on an annual basis to
  evaluate the salary progression of protected class members.

Career ladders are developed in the classification system to
  promote upward mobility.

The new employee orientation program includes information on
  diversity.

The performance appraisal program is periodically audited for
  clustering effects, barriers, and the relatedness of performance
  measures to essential job functions.

Job descriptions identify essential functions and physical
  requirements of the job.

The promotion system is periodically evaluated for identification
  of potentially discriminatory barriers.

Exhibit 3 (*Continued*)

ACCESS	*Yes*	*No*	*Score*

Turnover is analyzed annually, and the turnover rates of
  protected classes are compared with overall turnover rates.

Exit interviews or exit surveys are conducted.

Supervisory, managerial, and department chair evaluations
  include criteria related to diversity.

Criteria for tenure and promotion are evaluated to ensure the
  absence of discriminatory barriers.

INSTITUTIONAL VALUES AND RECEPTIVITY

The institutional values (or mission) statement explicitly
  references diversity.

The institution's strategic plan includes objectives related to
  diversity.

The institution has assigned accountability to achieve progress
  in reaching goals of diversity and monitors progress annually.

The institution has a strategic diversity plan and a comprehensive
  approach to diversity.

Diversity links and pipelines have been developed between the
  institution and the local community.

The campus community is apprised of the short- and long-range
  goals designed to promote diversity.

Multicultural programming is supported by institutional funding.

The institution provides incentives and rewards to personnel and
  units for being effective in making diversity a high priority.

Staff development seminars and workshops are conducted to
  acquaint institutional personnel with the goals and procedures
  for creating a more diverse community on campus.

Recognition is provided for the accomplishments of diverse teams.

Diverse members of the campus community are included in
  campus committees.

Communication systems foster inclusion and reinforce the
  institution's commitment to workplace diversity.

Source: Chun, 2004.

An alternative approach to diversity measurement is to develop an organizational diagnosis that aligns the institutional architecture needed to accomplish institutional diversity goals with organizational strategy (Ulrich, 1997). Translating the framework proposed by Ulrich into the architecture needed for campus diversity includes the following elements on the scorecard: a *shared mind-set* related to diversity, required *competencies* to achieve diversity, consequence or *reward systems* to reach the goals, *governance* and organizational structure, *work processes* to support diversity, and *leadership* for diversity (Ulrich, 1997).

Finally, the annual affirmative action plan itself is a method of structural diversity assessment that can be used to identify units that have attained hiring goals in recruiting minorities and to provide incentives such as increased travel money to reward them (Ponterotto, 1990b). Because the affirmative action plan is essentially focused on compliance, a forward-looking affirmative action planning process can be developed that asks department heads and administrators to reflect prospectively on hiring, development, and retention for the coming academic year. The process of engagement and long-term thinking heightens awareness of what individual departments can do to promote diversity in a defined time period. Reinforcement of these plans by executives helps to ensure that the annual planning process for affirmative action is meaningful and aligned with institutional goals.

Retention and Beyond

Although diversity strategic plans provide the vision, structure, and momentum for change, professional development, leave and benefits programs, and policies that support the retention of women and minorities are critical elements of the overall diversity strategy. A comprehensive range of policies includes work/family programs, leave policies or sabbaticals that deal with stopping the tenure clock for childbirth or adoption, benefit plans with provisions for domestic partners, flexible-time policies for staff, dual-career hiring, workload reduction programs, tuition waiver policies for families, and formal mentoring and professional development programs. In light of the breadth and depth of the rich body of literature, particularly in the area of work/family policies, that has emerged over the last decade, we highlight here only some of the key approaches and opportunities that may enhance the retention of diverse and talented faculty and staff.

A series of integrated policies that create a coherent framework for retention is preferable to discrete policy development (Ward and Wolf-Wendel, 2004).

The role of human resource practitioners is critical and a differentiating factor in institutions with family-friendly policies (see survey data compiled by Friedman, Rimsky, and Johnson, 1996, cited in Gappa and MacDermid, 1997).

A culture of fear can prevent the use of tenure extension policies by pretenure women faculty (Ward and Wolf-Wendel, 2004, Spalter-Roth and Erskine, 2005). Institutional safeguards may be needed to ensure that policies can be appropriately used.

Increased costs from the implementation of work-life and family-friendly programs are typically not significant, yet they have a highly positive overall effect in the perceived value of the total compensation package.

Consistency in the administration of programs and policies is essential to avoid the perception of favoritism. For example, Princeton University has pioneered a policy that makes extension of the tenure clock automatic in instances when a faculty member is giving birth to or adopting a child. This policy applies to both male and female faculty and has tripled the number of faculty members receiving the extension (Valdata, 2005).

To the extent that staff programs can provide flexibility similar to faculty programs, an institution can avoid the creation of two-tier systems.

Marketing family-friendly programs can heighten awareness of the specific benefits offered by the institution and provide a competitive edge in an intense labor market.

Campus advisory committees such as women's forums, gender equity committees, and diversity task forces can provide important input to the needs-assessment process in policy development.

From the perspective of recognizing, celebrating, and valuing diversity, institutional retention policies that ensure the success of women and minorities in the workplace provide an organizational safety net, promote optimal contributions and empowerment of members of the workforce, and help differentiate an institution as a "workplace of choice" in an intensely competitive labor market. For an institution to achieve a true culture of diversity, measurable actions must be taken and goals continually reevaluated to support diversity. An administrative infrastructure, strategic diversity planning, and assessment that guides diversity efforts ensure that institutional attention is continually focused on the work needed to advance and achieve genuine inclusion.

Reaching Reciprocal Empowerment: Recommendations and Implications

REPRESENTATIVE RESEARCH REVIEWED in this monograph indicates that substantial progress still needs to be made in higher education in the hiring, promotion, and retention of minority and women faculty and administrators. Over the last quarter century despite the existence of affirmative action, relatively small advances have been made in addressing the sheer demographic underrepresentation of minority faculty and administrators and only modest progress achieved by white females. Some danger may exist when the focus shifts to "diversity" without addressing the continuing structural underrepresentation of minorities. Further, in public research universities, a significant disparity persists between male and female faculty not only in demographic representation but also in the attainment of the highest faculty ranks.

Retention remains a major issue in reversing the phenomenon of the "revolving door." Institutional support mechanisms, human resource policies, and professional development programs focused on diversity and inclusion are needed to build shared understanding of the nature of systemic discrimination and to provide concerted, institutionwide approaches to change.

This monograph has examined how behavioral and organizational barriers hinder the career success of minorities and women in higher education and create patterns of exclusion, marginalization, and voicelessness. These patterns increase stress for minority and women faculty and administrators and have documented negative effects on their health and well-being. The deleterious and cumulative impact of stress deriving from perceived discrimination in the higher education workplace is only beginning to be understood and explored. Research on minority administrators also remains slim (Jackson, 2006).

Despite a thorough and exhaustive search of the literature, relatively little empirically based research exists regarding implementing models of empowerment in the higher education workplace. Perhaps this lack of empirical data results from the fact that comparatively few institutions have moved beyond affirmative action strategies to systematic institutional approaches that address the full participation of minorities and women.

Recent events in American politics suggest that race and gender have become less important on the national political scene with the election of the first black governor of Massachusetts, the selection of the first woman Speaker of the House, and the distinct possibility that a woman or African American could be candidates for the next president of the United States. *Washington Post* columnist David Broder (2007) writes perceptively of these recent events: "In neither case was the gender or race of the person competing for power the determinant of the outcome. Those who were deciding were able to look past these obvious characteristics to weigh their skills and leadership potential." Is the "color line" that W.E.B. DuBois described as the problem of the twentieth century eroding in this new century? (DuBois, 2005, p. 43).

Clearly much work still remains in higher education to ensure that race and gender do not determine outcomes in hiring, promotion, and retention. As a result, the importance of a conceptual framework to address these issues is paramount. As proposed in this monograph, the framework of reciprocal empowerment is an avenue that leads toward institutional transformation through engagement, mutuality, respect and recognition, and genuine inclusion in the workplace environment. The commitment of institutional leadership is an indispensable element in creating a climate and culture supportive of reciprocal empowerment and welcoming to diversity. As a champion of diversity change, leadership has the opportunity to provide the impetus and vision for these efforts, allocate resources, reward significant contributions, and ensure accountability.

Although public research universities have led the way in the creation and dissemination of diversity strategic plans, the actual measure of success of these plans depends on the attainment of concrete outcomes. Tangible results and measurable outcomes are needed to translate planning efforts into workplace realities. Without such results, the disconnect between diversity rhetoric and reality intensifies. Continued institutional attention and vigilance are required to erode the behavioral and organizational barriers to diversity identified in this monograph. The reallocation and appropriation of institutional resources for the development of diversity programs, incorporation of diversity issues in the curriculum, support for minority faculty leadership and participation in governance, and recognition of diversity service work are ways in which universities can transform organizational cultures to support diversity (Aguirre and Martinez, 2002).

How will universities know when reciprocal empowerment has been achieved or even is in progress? How will minority and female administrators and faculty know they have true allies? How can leadership clone successful models of reciprocal empowerment for institutionwide attention? Based on the discussion of behavioral and organizational barriers, certain questions can guide understanding of whether or not reciprocal empowerment is in evidence:

Structural representation. Has structural representation been attained for women and minority faculty and staff? Has representation been attained for executives, in governance structures, for department chairs, for administrative and academic leaders, among middle managers, and for professionals? Do recruitment efforts assist in changing patterns of structural underrepresentation? Have retention strategies helped ensure that minority and female faculty and staff stay at the university?

Mission, culture, and core values. Is diversity a core institutional value? If so, how is it measured, monitored, and implemented? Have rewards and recognition for diversity efforts been developed?

Institutional policies and processes. Are institutional safeguards in place to ensure that minority and female administrators and faculty are evaluated equitably in terms of expectations, contributions, and outcomes when compared with others in similar positions? Do policies and procedures reflect cohesive, state-of-the-art approaches to family and work life? Have programs for mentoring minority and female faculty and staff been implemented? Are significant professional development opportunities and opportunities for internal promotion or career growth made available to minorities and women? Does administrative succession planning include consideration of the growth potential of minorities and women?

Participation and decision making. Are minority and female administrators and faculty included in significant decision-making processes and governance? Is their decision-making ability commensurate with the level of their position and with the authority accorded to similarly situated positions? Are minorities and women represented at the table and are their contributions supported in the institutional hierarchy? Are minority and female faculty and staff engaged and empowered to add value?

Because reciprocal empowerment addresses the quality of interaction in the academic workplace, it fosters a climate that promotes retention and career satisfaction. Through the insights gained from an exploration of twenty-first-century organizational and behavioral barriers to diversity, a clearer view of the model of reciprocal empowerment emerges. Reciprocal empowerment gives voice to minority and female faculty and administrators through enhancing collaboration and participation. It promotes the formation, development, and expression of professional identity by valuing, embracing, and celebrating differences. It decenters power and provides new models for organizational decision making. It fosters a workplace for faculty and staff characterized by respect and recognition. Reciprocal empowerment is the conceptual framework that can promote the realization of a culture of equity and inclusion in higher education, fulfilling W.E.B. DuBois's vision of the university as the connection between the knowledge of life and the reality of life.

Appendix: Representative Diversity Strategic Plans and Diversity Web Sites for Public Research Universities

Institution	Type*	Enrollment	Title/Date	Best Practices
Auburn University (Auburn, Alabama) http://web6.duc.auburn.edu/administration/specialreports/diversity_plan/diversityplanfinal.pdf	RU/H	22,928	Strategic Diversity Plan, 2005	Establishes five strategic diversity goals, each with multiple strategies subdivided into tactics, partners, and measures. Creates a career development and succession planning program through partnerships of the Human Resources office, Provost's office, Women's Leadership Program, and Career Development Services. Identifies mentoring programs for both faculty and staff. Includes diversity as a performance dimension in evaluations for all faculty, administrators, and staff. Develops Communication Plan for Diversity.
Indiana University (Bloomington, Indiana) http://www.iub.edu/~asd/diversity/2020–2003.pdf	RU/VH	37,821	20/20: A Vision for Achieving Equity and Excellence at IU–Bloomington, 2003	Documents progress in achieving diversity goals over the past five years with an emphasis on minority student enrollment. Outcomes achieved include the establishment of a joint position of vice chancellor for academic support and diversity/university vice president for student development and diversity and diversity hires made through the strategic hiring and support program. Addresses travel funds and other retention initiatives for minority faculty.

(Continued)

Appendix: (Continued)

Institution	Type*	Enrollment	Title/Date	Best Practices
Kent State University (Kent, Ohio) http://www.kent.edu/diversity/upload/Diversity%20Plan.pdf	RU/H	24,347	Diversity Implementation Plan, 2001–2005: A Framework to Foster Diversity in Kent State's Eight-Campus System	Creates a framework to foster diversity in eight-campus system. Addresses recruitment, retention, and enrollment management with multiple goals and strategies.
Ohio State University (Columbus, Ohio) www.osu.edu/diversity/council_report.html and http://www.osu.edu/diversity/docs/analysis2004–2005.pdf	RU/VH	50,995	Diversity Action Plan, 2000; Diversity Plans: An Analysis 2004–2005	Identifies six primary objectives with accountability for each objective and generates report card based on the diversity action plan. Identifies funding for specific diversity-related initiatives. Includes comprehensive report of the progress of all divisions, colleges, and schools in attaining plan goals.
Pennsylvania State University (University Park, Pennsylvania) http://www.equity.psu.edu/framework/assets/framework_to_foster_div.pdf	RU/VH	41,289	A Framework to Foster Diversity, 2004–2009	Builds on seven challenges identified in a prior five-year plan using a framework for research on diversity derived from Smith (1995) that addresses the dimensions of campus climate and intergroup relations, access and success, education and scholarship, and institutional viability and vitality. Uses evaluation teams of key stakeholders for midpoint review and updates demographic

Institution		Enrollment	Document	Description
University of Arizona, Tucson (Tucson, Arizona) http://diversity.arizona.edu	RU/VH	36,932	Diversity Action Plan, 2003	data profiles at midpoint and final assessment. Identifies target areas for improvement for each challenge and assessment questions. Establishes priorities, specific action steps, and responsibilities. Created Diversity Resource Office in 2003 to advance diversity initiatives. Addresses retention and mentoring. Includes campus climate assessments for underrepresented groups and lesbian, gay, and transgender persons.
University of California at Los Angeles (Los Angeles, California) http://www.diversity.ucla.edu	RU/VH	35,966	Diversity@UCLA	Web site includes extensive faculty diversity web and resources for faculty searches, family policy, diversity resources, affirmative action, and gender equity. Web site also includes an assessment of the academic climate for faculty completed in 2003.
University of California at San Diego (San Diego, California) http://diversity.ucsd.edu	RU/VH	24,663	Diversity Matters (Web site)	Includes short-, intermediate-, and longer-term initiatives with recommendations for incentives to implement changes to organizational structures and work models.

(Continued)

Appendix: (Continued)

Institution	Type*	Enrollment	Title/Date	Best Practices
University of Colorado at Boulder (Boulder, Colorado) http://www.colorado.edu/cu-diversity/blueprint	RU/VH	32,362	Campus Diversity Plan: A Blueprint for Action, 1999	References action of CU board of regents to approve diversity plan for each of CU's four campuses in response to mandate from Colorado Commission on Higher Education for public universities to create campus diversity plans. References diversity goals in three broad areas: climate for living, learning, and working; student access and opportunity; and diverse faculty and staff.
University of Louisville (Louisville, Kentucky) http://www.louisville.edu/provost/diversity/localresources/images/DiversityPlan.pdf	RU/H	21,750	Achieving Our Highest Potential: Diversity Plan for the University of Louisville, 2003	Creates a diversity plan monitoring task force to review progress toward diversity goals. Evaluates all deans and vice presidents on performance in implementing diversity unit plans. Requires each unit to submit a diversity plan linked to the strategic plan. Unit plans must include action steps, accountability, timetable of outcomes, and assessment. Sets aggressive targets for institutionwide minority recruitment.
University of Maryland (College Park, Maryland) http://www.inform.umd.edu/EdRes/Topic/Diversity	RU/VH	34,993	Diversity database syllabi	Includes diversity resources, institutional diversity initiatives, and diversity-related syllabi.

University of Massachusetts at Amherst (Amherst, Massachusetts) http://www.umass.edu/campusdiversity/pdfs/final_report.pdf	RU/H	24,646	Diversity and Inclusion at UMass Amherst: A Blueprint for Change, 2005	Describes the importance of systemic efforts to improve diversity as well as preventive (planning-centered) rather than reactive (crisis-oriented) modes of addressing diversity. Emphasizes inclusion and empowerment. Recommends establishment of incentives and rewards for individuals and units undertaking special efforts to implement university diversity goals. Identifies importance of benchmarks and planning targets.
University of New Hampshire (Durham, New Hampshire) http://www.unh.edu/diversity/pdf/DiversityPlan.pdf	RU/VH	14,370	Diversity Strategic Plan, 2004–2009	Identifies seven comprehensive strategies to be implemented in four years and assessed in 2009. Strategies fall into five categories: organizational structure, recruitment and retention, curriculum, climate, and outreach and engagement. Addresses accountability and timelines for progress reports.
University of South Florida (Lakeland, Florida) http://web1.cas.usf.edu/MAIN/include/0-1201-004/diversity_plan.pdf?CFID=873294&CFTOKEN=55347328	RU/VH	42,238	Strategic Diversity Plan, 2005 (with goals identified as CLEAR: Climate, Leadership, Excellence, Access, and Representation)	Describes faculty enrichment program and incentives for hiring women and minorities. Discusses results of 2002 Campus Climate Survey, to which 1,827 employees responded.

(Continued)

Appendix: (Continued)

Institution	Type*	Enrollment	Title/Date	Best Practices
University of Washington (Seattle, Washington) http://depts.washington.edu/divinit/UW%20 Diversity%20Apprais al%20revised.pdf	RU/VH	39,199	Diversity Appraisal	Collates diversity appraisal reports from three campuses and addresses questions relating to diversity in curriculum, research, climate, faculty diversity, staff and administrative diversity, engagement with external community, student access and opportunities, and student development and retention. A fund of $400,000 was allocated over two years for diversity initiatives. Best Practices working groups provide opportunities for interinstitutional learning.
University of Wisconsin at Madison (Madison, Wisconsin) http:// www.provost.wisc. edu/docs/plan2008. pdf	RU/VH	40,455	Plan 2008 (2003–2008)	Follows University of Wisconsin System Design for Diversity and plans developed at Madison in 1988 and 1993. Contains recommendations in seven broad areas. Specific goals for improving representation and academic success of four targeted ethnic groups: American Indian, African American, Latino and Latina, and Southeast Asian American. Strategic hiring fund of $1 million annually for high-priority faculty hires (women and underrepresented minorities as well as dual-career couples).

| Virginia Polytechnic Institute and State University (Blacksburg, Virginia) http://www.dsp.multicultural.vt.edu/pdfs/DSP-All.pdf | RU/VH | 27,619 | University Diversity Plan, 2000–2005 | Aligns with "Implementation Plan of the Academic Agenda" and the university's six strategic directions. Includes measures, accountability, time line, and tasks for each goal. Goals are directed toward improving structural diversity, climate, education and training, responsibility, accountability and recognition, and internal and external collaborations and partnerships. |
| Washington State University (Pullman, Washington) http://diversity.wsu.edu/Templates/strategic%20plan%20021405.asp | RU/VH | 18,690 | Framework for the University Strategic Plan for Equity and Diversity, 2005 | Includes strategic goals and benchmarks. |

*Carnegie Basic Classification: RU/VH: Research University (very high research activity) RU/H: Research University (high research activity).

References

Academic Quality Improvement Project. (2002). *Principles and criteria for improving academic quality.* Retrieved September 18, 2005, from http://www.iun.edu/~spcnw/Outcome5/ Principles_CriteriaBooklet.pdf.

Aguirre, A., Jr. (2000). *Women and minority faculty in the academic workplace: Recruitment, retention, and academic culture.* ASHE-ERIC Higher Education Report, Vol. 27, No. 6. San Francisco: Jossey-Bass.

Aguirre, A., Jr., and Martinez, R. O. (1993). *Chicanos in higher education: Issues and dilemmas for the twenty-first century.* ASHE-ERIC Higher Education Report, Vol. 22, No. 3. Washington, DC: School of Education and Human Development, George Washington University.

Aguirre, A., Jr., and Martinez, R. O. (2002). Leadership practices and diversity in higher education: Transitional and transformational frameworks. *Journal of Leadership Studies, 8*(3), 53–62.

Aguirre, A., Jr., and Martinez, R. O. (2007). *Diversity leadership in higher education.* ASHE-ERIC Higher Education Report, Vol. 32, No. 3. San Francisco: Jossey-Bass.

Aguirre, A., Jr., and Turner, J. H. (1998). *American ethnicity: The dynamics and consequences of discrimination* (2nd ed.). Boston: McGraw-Hill.

Allison, K. (1998). Stress and oppressed social category membership. In J. K. Swim and C. Stangor (Eds.), *Prejudice: The target's perspective* (pp. 145–170). San Diego: Academic Press.

American Association of University Professors. (1966). *Statement on government of colleges and universities.* Retrieved June 9, 2005, from http://www.aaup.org/statements/Redbook/ Govern.htm.

American Council on Education, Office of Women in Higher Education. (2005). *An agenda for excellence: Creating flexibility in tenure-track faculty careers.* Retrieved August 28, 2006, from http://www.acenet.edu/bookstore/pdf /2005_tenure_flex_summary.pdf.

Antokoviak, E. (2004). The interrelationship between affirmative action and diversity. Unpublished figure.

Antonio, A. L. (2002). Faculty of color reconsidered: Reassessing contributions to scholarship. *Journal of Higher Education, 73*(5), 582–602.

Arveson, P. (1998). *What is the balanced scorecard?* Retrieved September 12, 2005, from http://www.balancedscorecard.org/basics/bsc1.html.

Auburn University. (2005). *Strategic diversity plan.* Retrieved June 12, 2006, from http://web6.duc.auburn.edu/administration/specialreports/diversity_plan/diversityplanfinal.pdf.

Austin, A. E., Rice, R. E., and Splete, A. P. (1991). *A good place to work: Sourcebook for the academic workplace.* Washington, DC: Council of Independent Colleges.

Baez, B. (2002). Affirmative action, hate speech, and tenure: Narratives about race, law, and the academy. New York: Routledge Falmer.

Baez, B., and Centra, J. A. (1995). *Tenure, promotion, and reappointment: Legal and administrative implications.* ASHE-ERIC Higher Education Report, Vol. 24, No. 1. Washington, DC: Graduate School of Education and Development, George Washington University.

Bar-Tal, D. (1989). Delegitimization: The extreme case of stereotyping and prejudice. In D. Bar-Tal, C. Grauman, A. Kruglanski, and W. Stroege (Eds.), *Stereotyping and prejudice: Changing conceptions* (pp. 169–182). New York: Springer-Verlag.

Bartky, S. L. (1990). *Femininity and domination: Studies in the phenomenology of oppression.* New York: Routledge.

Basinger, J. (2002). Casting a wider net. Colleges are more likely to find presidents outside academe: Most chiefs are still white men. *Chronicle of Higher Education, 49*(16), A32–A33. Retrieved June 16, 2005, from http://chronicle.com/weekly/v49/i16/16a03201.htm.

Becker, B. E., Huselid, M. A., and Ulrich, D. (2001). *The HR scorecard: Linking people, strategy, and performance.* Boston: Harvard Business School Press.

Bell, L. A. (1997). Theoretical foundations for social justice education. In M. Adams, L. A. Bell, and P. Griffin (Eds.), *Teaching for diversity and social justice: A sourcebook* (pp. 3–15). New York: Routledge.

Bensimon, E. M. (2004). The diversity scorecard: A learning approach to institutional change. *Change, 36*(1), 44–52.

Bertrand, M., and Mullainathan, S. (2004). Are Emily and Greg more employable than Lakisha and Jamal? A field experiment on labor market discrimination. *American Economic Review, 94*(4), 991–1014.

Bettencourt, B. A., and Miller, N. (1996). Gender differences in aggression as a function of provocation: A meta-analysis. *Psychological Bulletin, 119*(3), 422–447.

Blackburn, R. T., and Lawrence, J. H. (1995). *Faculty at work: Motivation, expectation, satisfaction.* Baltimore: Johns Hopkins University Press.

Blackwell, J. E. (1996). Faculty issues: The impact on minorities. In C. S. Turner, M. Garcia, A. Nora, and L. I. Redon (Eds.), *Racial and ethnic diversity in higher education* (pp. 315–326). Needham Heights, MA: Simon & Schuster.

Blakemore, J.E.O., Switzer, J. Y., DiLorio, J. A., and Fairchild, D. L. (1997). Exploring the campus climate for women faculty. In N. V. Benokraitis (Ed.), *Subtle sexism: Current practice and prospects for change* (pp. 54–72). Thousand Oaks, CA: Sage.

Boice, R. (1993). Early turning points in professorial careers of women and minorities. In J. Gainen and R. Boice (Eds.), *Building a diverse faculty.* New Directions for Teaching and Learning, no. 53, pp. 71–80. San Francisco: Jossey-Bass.

116

Boyer, E. L. (1990). Scholarship reconsidered: Priorities of the professoriate. Princeton, NJ: Carnegie Foundation for the Advancement of Teaching.

Bradburn, E. M., Skora, A. C., and Zimbler, U. J. (2002). *Gender and racial/ethnic differences in salary and other characteristics of postsecondary faculty: Fall 1998.* Statistical analysis report. Retrieved September 17, 2006, from http://nces.ed. gov/pubs2002/ 2002170.pdf.

Britt, R. R. (2006). *Life expectancy in America hits record high.* Retrieved July 8, 2005, from http://www.livescience.com/humanbiology/050228_life_expectancy.html.

Brockbank, W. (2004). *The essence of great workplaces. Interview with Wayne Brockbank: Only externally focused cultures will thrive.* Retrieved April 9, 2006, from http://www.growtalent.com/gptw/interview.htm.

Broder, D. S. (2007, January 7). The ebb of prejudice. *The Washington Post.* Retrieved January 7, 2007, from http://www.washingtonpost.com.

Bronstein, P. (1993). Challenges, rewards, and costs for feminist and ethnic minority scholars. In J. Gainen and R. Boyce (Eds.), *Building a diverse faculty.* New Directions for Teaching and Learning, no. 53, pp. 61–70. San Francisco: Jossey-Bass.

Bronstein, P., and Farnsworth, L. (1998). Gender differences in faculty experiences of interpersonal climate and processes for advancement. *Research in Higher Education, 39*(5), 557–586.

Bronstein, P., and Ramaley, J. A. (2002). Making the persuasive tenure case: Pitfalls and possibilities. In J. E. Cooper and D. D. Stevens (Eds.), *Tenure in the sacred grove: Issues and strategies for women and minority faculty* (pp. 31–55). Albany: State University of New York Press.

Busenberg, B. E., and Smith, D. G. (1997). Affirmative action and beyond: The woman's perspective. In M. Garcia (Ed.), *Affirmative action's testament of hope: Strategies for a new era in higher education* (pp. 149–180). Albany: State University of New York Press.

Catalyst. (1999). *Women in color in corporate management: Opportunities and barriers.* New York: Catalyst.

Chandler, D. L. (1993). Incorporating diversity into the professoriate. In L. Richlin (Ed.), *Preparing faculty for the new conceptions of scholarship* (pp. 91–101). San Francisco: Jossey-Bass.

Chase, S. E. (1995). *Ambiguous empowerment: The work narratives of women school superintendents.* Amherst: University of Massachusetts Press.

Chun, E. (2004). *Sample diversity scorecard.* Paper presented at a meeting of the College and University Professional Association for Human Resources, May, Newport, RI.

Clark, R., Anderson, N. B., Clark, V. R., and Williams, D. R. (1999). Racism as a stressor for African Americans: A biopsychosocial model. *American Psychologist, 4*(10), 805–816.

Clayton-Pedersen, A., and Musil, C. M. (2005). *Introduction to the series.* Retrieved May 15, 2006, from http://www.aacu.org/inclusive_excellence/documents/Williams_et_al.pdf.

Cohen, S., Kessler, R., and Gordon, L. (1995). *Measuring stress: A guide for health and social scientists.* New York: Oxford University Press.

Collins, P. H. (1993). Learning from the outsider within: The sociological significance of black feminist thought. In J. S. Glazer-Raymo, E. M. Bensimon, and B. K. Townsend (Eds.), *Women in higher education: A feminist perspective* (pp. 45–64). Needham Heights, MA: Ginn Press.

Cooper, J., and Stevens, D. D. (Eds.). (2002a). *Tenure in the sacred grove: Issues and strategies for women and minority faculty.* Albany: State University of New York Press.

Cooper, J., and Stevens, D. D. (2002b). The journey towards tenure. In J. Cooper and D. D. Stevens (Eds.), *Tenure in the sacred grove: Issues and strategies for women and minority faculty* (pp. 3–16). Albany: State University of New York Press.

Cooper, R. S. (1993). Health and the social status of blacks in the United States. *Annals of Epidemiology, 3*(2), 137–144.

Corning, A. F. (2002). Self-esteem as a moderator between perceived discrimination and psychological distress among women. *Journal of Counseling Psychology, 49*(1), 117–126.

Crocker, J., and Major, B. (1989). Social stigma and self-esteem: The self-protective properties of stigma. *Psychological Review, 96*(4), 608–630.

Crocker, J., Vole, K., Test, M., and Major, B. (1991). Social stigma: The affective consequences of attributional ambiguity. *Journal of Personality and Social Psychology, 60*(2), 218–228.

Crosby, F. J. (2004). *Affirmative action is dead: Long live affirmative action.* New Haven, CT: Yale University Press.

Cross, E. Y. (1992). Making the invisible visible. *Healthcare Forum Journal, 35*(1), 28–32.

Cross, T., and Slater, B. (2002). A short list of colleges and universities that are taking measures to increase their number of black faculty. *Journal of Blacks in Higher Education, 36*, 99–104.

Curry, B. K. (2002). The caged bird sings: On being different and the role of advocacy. In J. Cooper and D. D. Stevens (Eds.), *Tenure in the sacred grove: Issues and strategies for women and minority faculty* (pp. 117–126). Albany: State University of New York Press.

Darlington, P.S.E., and Mulvaney, B. M. (2003). *Women, power, and ethnicity: Working toward reciprocal empowerment.* Binghamton, NY: Haworth Press.

Deitch, E. A., and others. (2003). Subtle yet significant: The existence and impact of everyday racial discrimination in the workplace. *Human Relations, 56*(11), 1299–1324.

de la Luz Reyes, M., and Halcon, J. J. (1988). Racism in academia: The old wolf revisited. *Harvard Educational Review, 58*(3), 299–314.

DeVries, D. L. (1975). The relationship of role expectations to faculty behavior. *Research in Higher Education, 3*, 111–129.

Dey, E. L. (1994). Dimensions of faculty stress: A recent survey. *Review of Higher Education, 17*(3), 305–322.

Diamond, R. (1993). Instituting change in the faculty reward system. In R. M. Diamond and B. E. Adam (Eds.), *Recognizing faculty work: Reward systems for the year 2000* (pp. 13–22). San Francisco: Jossey-Bass.

Douglass, F. (1857). *The Frederick Douglass papers.* Retrieved February 19, 2006, from http://www.buildingequality.us/Quotes/Frederick_Douglass.htm.

Dovidio, J. F., Gaertner, S. L., and Bachman, B. A. (2001). Racial bias in organizations: The role of group processes in its causes and cures. In M. Turner (Ed.), *Groups at work: Theory and research* (pp. 415–444). Mahwah, NJ: Erlbaum.

DuBois, W.E.B. (2005). *The souls of black folk.* New York: Pocket Books.

Dugger, K. (2001). Women in higher education in the United States: Has there been progress?. *International Journal of Sociology and Social Policy, 21*(1/2), 118–130.

Eckel, P. D., and Kezar, A. J. (2003). *Taking the reins: Institutional transformation in higher education.* Westport, CT: Praeger.

Ehrenberg, R. G., Klaff, D. B., Kezsbom, A. T., and Nagowski, M. P. (2004). Collective bargaining in American higher education. In R. G. Ehrenberg (Ed.), *Governing academia* (pp. 209–232). Ithaca, NY: Cornell University Press.

Elliott, J. R., and Smith, R. A. (2004). Race, gender, and workplace power. *American Sociological Review, 69*(3), 365–386.

Ellison, R. (1995). *Invisible man* (2nd ed.). New York: Random House.

Faces of change: University diversity plan, 2000–2005. (2000). Retrieved June 12, 2006, from http://www. dsp.multicultural.vt.edu/pdfs/DSP-All.pdf.

Faculty strategic hiring initiative, 2006–2007. (2006). University of Wisconsin Madison. Retrieved August 28, 2006, from http://www.provost.wisc.edu/hiring/facshi.html.

Fairweather, J. S. (1996). Faculty work and public trust: Restoring the value of teaching and public service in American academic life. Boston: Allyn & Bacon.

Feagin, J. R. (2001). *Racist America: Roots, current realities, and future reparations.* New York: Routledge.

Feagin, J. R., and McKinney, K. D. (2003). *The many costs of racism.* Lanham, MD: Rowman & Littlefield.

Feagin, J. R., and O'Brien, E. (2003). *White men on race: Power, privilege, and the shaping of cultural consciousness.* Boston: Beacon Press.

Feagin, J. R., and Sikes, M. P. (1994). *Living with racism: The black middle-class experience.* Boston: Beacon Press.

Feagin, J. R., Vera, H., and Imani, N. (1996). *The agony of education: Black students at white colleges and universities.* London: Routledge.

Finkelstein, M. J., Seal, R. K., and Schuster, J. H. (1998). *The new academic generation: A profession in transformation.* Baltimore: Johns Hopkins University Press.

Fontaine, D. C., and Greenlee, S. P. (1993). Black women: Double solos in the workplace. *Western Journal of Black Studies, 17*(3), 121–125.

Freire, P. (1970). *Pedagogy of the oppressed.* New York: Herder & Herder.

Friedman, D. E., Rimsky, C., and Johnson, A. A. (1996). *College and university reference guide to work-family programs: Report on a collaborative study.* New York: Families and Work Institute.

Friedman, T. L. (2005). *The world is flat: A brief history of the twenty-first century.* New York: Farrar, Straus & Giroux.

Gaertner, S. L., and Dovidio, J. F. (2000). The aversive form of racism. In C. Stangor (Ed.), *Stereotypes and prejudice: Essential readings* (pp. 289–304). Philadelphia: Psychology Press.

Gappa, J. M., and MacDermid, S. (1997). *Work, family, and the faculty career.* Washington, DC: American Association for Higher Education.

Garcia, M., and others. (2001). *Assessing campus diversity initiatives: A guide for campus practitioners.* Washington, DC: Association of American Colleges and Universities.

Gardenswartz, L., and Rowe, A. (1994). *The managing diversity survival guide: A complete collection of checklists, activities, and tips.* Boston: McGraw-Hill.

Glazer-Raymo, J. (1999). *Shattering the myths: Women in academe.* Baltimore: Johns Hopkins University Press.

Goodman, D. (2001). *Promoting diversity and social justice: Educating people from privileged groups.* Thousand Oaks, CA: Sage.

Granger, M. W. (1993). A review of the literature on the status of women and minorities in the professoriate in higher education. *Journal of School Leadership, 3*(2), 121–135.

Graumann, C. F., and Wintermantel, M. (1989). Discriminatory speech acts: A functional approach. In D. Bar-Tal, C. F. Graumann, A. W. Kruglanski, and W. Stroebe (Eds.), *Sterotyping and prejudice: Changing conceptions* (pp. 184–204). New York: Springer-Verlag.

Graves, S. B. (1990). A case of double jeopardy? Black women in higher education. *Initiatives, 53*(1), 3–8.

Green, C. E., and King, V. G. (2001). Sisters mentoring sisters: Africentric leadership development for black women in the academy. *Journal of Negro Education, 70*(3), 156–165.

Greenhaus, J. H., and Parasuraman, S. (1993). Job performance attributions and career advancement prospects: An examination of gender and race effects. *Organizational Behavior and Human Decision Processes, 55*(2), 273–297.

Gregory, A. (2003). Black and female in the academy. *Chronicle of Higher Education, 49*(39), C5.

Gregory, S. T. (2001). Black faculty women in the academy: History, status, and future. *Journal of Negro Education, 70*(3), 124–138.

Gurin, P., Dey, E. L., Hurtado, S., and Gurin, G. (2002). Diversity and higher education: Theory and impact on educational outcomes. *Harvard Educational Review, 72*(3), 330–366.

Hammond, T. H. (2004). Herding cats in university hierarchies: Formal structure and policy choice in American research universities. In R. G. Ehrenberg (Ed.), *Governing academia* (pp. 91–138). Ithaca, NY: Cornell University Press.

Hardiman, R., and Jackson, B. W. (1997). Conceptual foundation for social justice courses. In M. Adams, L. A. Bell, and P. Griffin (Eds.), *Teaching for diversity and social justice: A sourcebook* (pp. 16–29). New York: Routledge.

Harvey, W. B., and Anderson, E. L. (2005). *Minorities in higher education: 2003–2004. Twenty-first annual status report.* Washington, DC: American Council on Education.

Haub, C. (2006). *Hispanics account for almost one-half of U.S. population growth.* Retrieved July 11, 2006, from http://www.prb.org/Template.cfm?Section=PRB&template=/Content Management/ContentDisplay.cfm&ContentID=13604.

Hubbard, E. E. (2004). *The diversity scorecard: Evaluating the impact of diversity on organizational performance.* Burlington, MA: Elsevier Butterworth-Heinemann.

Humphreys, D. (2000). Diversity plan trends aim to meet 21st century challenges: The current generation of diversity plans seek to be more inclusive—and we're not just talking about numerically. *Black Issues in Higher Education, 16*(25), 34–36.

Hurtado, S. (1996). The campus racial climate: Contexts of conflict. In C.S.V. Turner, M. Garcia, A. Nora, and L. I. Redon (Eds.), *Racial and ethnic diversity in higher education* (pp. 485–506). Needham Heights, MA: Simon & Schuster.

Hurtado, S., Milem, J., Clayton-Pedersen, A., and Allen, W. (1999). *Enacting diverse learning environments: Improving the climate for racial/ethnic diversity in higher education*. ASHE-ERIC Higher Education Report, Vol. 26, No. 8. Washington, DC: Graduate School of Education and Human Development, George Washington University.

Huselid, M. A., Becker, B. E., and Beatty, R. W. (2005). *The workforce scorecard: Managing human capital to execute strategies*. Boston: Harvard Business School Press.

Ibarra, H. (1995). Race, opportunity, and diversity of social circles in managerial networks. *Academy of Management Journal, 38*(3), 673–704.

"Implementing hiring for diversity: Supplement 1A to university affirmative action report." (n.d.). Retrieved August 29, 2006, from http://www.kent.edu/diversity/DiversityInstruments/Instruments.cfm.

Jackson, J.F.L. (2006). Hiring practices of African American males in academic leadership positions at American colleges and universities: An employment trends and disparate impact analysis. *Teachers College Record, 108*(2), 316–338.

Jackson, K. W. (1991). Black faculty in academia. In P. G. Altbach and K. Lomotey (Eds.), *The racial crisis in American higher education* (pp. 135–165). Albany: State University of New York Press.

Jackson, P. B., and Mustillo, S. (2001). I am woman: The impact of social identities on African American women's mental health. *Women and Health, 32*(4), 33–59.

Jaschik, S. (1991). Hundreds weigh in on accrediting group's "diversity standard." *Chronicle of Higher Education, 37*(48), A17–A18.

Jaschik, S. (1992). Education Dept. report recommends recognition for Middle States group. *Chronicle of Higher Education, 38*(19), A30.

Johnson, B. J., and Harvey, W. (2002). The socialization of black college faculty: Implications for policy and practice. *Review of Higher Education, 25*(3), 297–314.

Johnsrud, L. K. (1996). *Maintaining morale: A guide to assessing the morale of midlevel administrators and faculty*. Washington, DC: College and Personnel Association.

Johnsrud, L. K., and Des Jarlais, C. D. (1994). Barriers to tenure for women and minorities. *Review of Higher Education, 17*(4), 335–353.

Johnsrud, L. K., and Heck, R. H. (1994). Administrative promotion within a university: The cumulative impact of gender. *Journal of Higher Education, 65*(1), 23–44.

Johnsrud, L. K., and Sadao, K. C. (1998). The common experience of otherness: Ethnic and racial minority faculty. *Review of Higher Education, 21*(4), 315–342.

Kanter, R. M. (1977). *Men and women of the corporation*. New York: Basic Books.

Kennedy, J. F. (1963, February). *Affirmative action: An historical perspective in Los Angeles County government*. Retrieved June 7, 2006, from http://oaac.co.la.ca.us/ AAMain.shtml.

Kerner Commission. (1968). *Report of the national commission on civil disorder*. New York: Bantam Books.

Kessler, R. C., Mickelson, K. D., and Williams, D. R. (1999). The prevalence, distribution, and mental health correlates of perceived discrimination in the United States. *Journal of Health and Social Behavior, 40*(3), 208–230.

Kilian, C. M., Hukai, D., and McCarty, C. E. (2005). Building diversity in the pipeline to corporate leadership. *Journal of Management Development, 24*(2), 155–168.

Kincheloe, J., and Steinberg, D. (1998). Addressing the crisis of whiteness: Reconfiguring white identity in a pedagogy of whiteness. In J. L. Kincheloe, S. R. Steinberg, N. M. Rodriguez, and R. E. Chennault (Eds.), *White reign: Deploying whiteness in America* (pp. 3–29). New York: St. Martin's Press.

Knox, M., and Teraguchi, D. H. (2005). Institutional models that cultivate comprehensive change. *Diversity Digest, 9*(2), 10–11.

Konrad, A. M., and Pfeffer, J. (1996). Understanding the hiring of women and minorities in educational institutions. In C.S.V. Turner, M. Garcia, A. Nora, and L. I. Redon (Eds.), *Racial and ethnic diversity in higher education* (pp. 507–525). Needham Heights, MA: Simon & Schuster.

Kramer, G. R. (1982). Title VII on campus: Judicial review of university employment decisions. *Columbia Law Review, 82*(6), 1206–1235.

Krieger, N., and Sidney, S. (1996). Racial discrimination and blood pressure: The CARDIA study of young black and white adults. *American Journal of Public Health, 86*(10), 1370–1378.

Kuh, G. D., and Whitt, E. J. (1988). *The invisible tapestry: Culture in American colleges and universities.* ASHE-ERIC Higher Education Report, No. 1. Washington, DC: Graduate School of Education and Human Development, George Washington University.

Kulis, S. (1997). Gender segregation among college and university employees. *Sociology of Education, 70*(2), 151–173.

Kulis, S., Chong, Y., and Shaw, H. (1999). Discriminatory organizational contexts and black scientists on postsecondary faculties. *Research in Higher Education, 40*(2), 115–148.

Leap, T. L. (1995). *Tenure, discrimination, and the courts* (2nd ed.). Ithaca, NY: ILR Press.

Leatherman, C. (1991). West Coast accrediting agency hashes out a policy on racial diversity for campuses. *Chronicle of Higher Education, 39*(13), A15–A16.

Ledford, G. E., Jr. (2002). *Attracting, retaining, and motivating employees: The rewards of work framework.* Paper presented at a meeting of the College and University Professional Association for Human Resources, October, Dallas, TX.

Levin, R. (2006, August 21). *Universities branch out: From their student bodies to their research practices, universities are becoming more global.* Retrieved December 22, 2006, from http://www.law.yale.edu/documents/pdf/Public_Affairs/PresidentLevinArticle.pdf.

Lima, M. (2003). If not now, then when? Unpublished manuscript, State University of New York at Geneseo.

Lindholm, J. A., Szelenyi, K., Hurtado, S., and Korn, W. S. (2005). The American college teacher: National norms for the 2004–2005 HERI faculty survey. Los Angeles: Higher Education Research Institute, University of California, Los Angeles.

Lindsay, B. (1994). African American women and Brown: A lingering twilight or emerging dawn? *Journal of Negro Education, 63*(3), 430–442.

Loden, M., and Rosener, J. B. (1991). *Workforce America! Managing employee diversity as a vital resource.* Homewood, IL: Business One Irwin.

Marschke, R., Laursen, S., Nielsen, J. M., and Rankin, P. (2007). Demographic inertia revisited: An immodest proposal to achieve equitable gender representation among faculty in higher education. *Journal of Higher Education, 78*(1), 1–26.

Martin, J. (1994). Recent developments concerning accrediting agencies in postsecondary education. *Law and Contemporary Problems, 57*(4), 121–149.

McDonough, P. M. (2002). Resisting common injustice: Tenure politics, department politics, gay and lesbian politics. In J. Cooper and D. D. Stevens (Eds.), *Tenure in the sacred grove: Issues and strategies for women and minority faculty* (pp. 127–147). Albany: State University of New York Press.

Milem, J. F., and Astin, H. S. (1993). The changing composition of the faculty: What does it mean for diversity? *Change, 25*(2), 21–27.

Milem, J. F., Chang, M. J., and Antonio, A. L. (2005). *Making diversity work on campus: A research-based perspective.* Retrieved May 24, 2006, from http://www.aft.org/pubs-reports/higher_ed/shared_governance.pdf.

Minor, J. T., and Tierney, W. G. (2005). The danger of deference: A case of polite governance. *Teachers College Record, 107*(1), 137–156.

Minority faculty recruitment resources and guidelines. (2006). Retrieved December 20, 2005, from http://www.hreo.ku.edu/employment/recruitment search_processes/recruitment_guidelines/diversity_strategy.shtml.

Moore, W., Jr. (1987). Black faculty in white colleges: A dream deferred. *Educational Record, 68*(4), 116–121.

Moreno, J. F., and others. (2006). *The revolving door for underrepresented minority faculty in higher education: An analysis from the Campus Diversity Initiative.* Retrieved April 26, 2006, from http://www.irvine.org/assets/pdf/pubs/education/insight_Revolving_Dooor.pdf.

Musil, C. M., and others. (1999). *To form a more perfect union: Campus diversity initiatives.* Washington, DC: Association of American Colleges and Universities.

Myers, H. F., Lewis, T. T., and Parker-Dominguez, T. (2003). Stress, coping and minority health: Biopsychosocial perspective on ethnic health disparities. In G. Bernal, J. E. Trimble, A. K. Burlew, and F. T. Leong (Eds.), *Handbook of racial and ethnic minority psychology* (pp. 377–400). Thousand Oaks, CA: Sage.

Myers, S. L., Jr. (1997). Why diversity is a smoke screen for affirmative action. *Change, 29*(4), 24–32.

Nakanishi, D. T. (1996). Asian Pacific Americans in higher education: Faculty and administrative representation and tenure. In C.S.V. Turner, M. Garcia, A. Nora, and L. I. Redon (Eds.), *Racial and ethnic diversity in higher education* (pp. 370–375). Needham Heights, MA: Simon & Schuster Custom.

Nelson, D. J., and Rogers, D. C. (2004). *A national analysis of diversity in science and engineering faculties at research universities.* Retrieved July 6, 2006, from http://www.now.org/issues/diverse/diversity_report.pdf.

Nidiffer, J., and Bashaw, C. T. (Eds.). (2001). *Women administrators in higher education: Historical and contemporary perspectives.* Albany: State University of New York Press.

Niemann, Y. F. (1999). The making of a token: A case study of stereotype threat, stigma racism and tokenism in academe. *Frontiers, 20*(1), 111–126.

Niemann, Y. F. (2003). The psychology of tokenism: Psychosocial realities of faculty of color. In G. Bernal, J. E. Trimble, A. K. Burlew, and F.T.L. Leong (Eds.), *Handbook of racial and ethnic minority psychology* (pp. 100–118). Thousand Oaks, CA: Sage.

O'Connor, S. D. (2003). Opinion of the court. In *Grutter* v. *Bollinger* et al. Retrieved July 13, 2005, from http://www.chronicle.com/free/documents/v49/i43/grutter.pdf.

Olsen, D., Maple, S. A., and Stage, F. K. (1995). Women and minority faculty job satisfaction: Professional role interests, professional satisfactions, and institutional fit. *Journal of Higher Education, 66*(3), 267–293.

Parham, T. A., and McDavis, R. J. (1987). Black men, an endangered species: Who's really pulling the trigger? *Journal of Counseling and Development, 66*, 24–27.

Park, S. M. (1996). Research, teaching, and service: Why shouldn't women's work count? *Journal of Higher Education, 67*(1), 46–84.

Patitu, C. L., and Hinton, H. G. (2003). The experiences of African American women faculty and administrators in higher education: Has anything changed? In M. F. Howard-Hamilton (Ed.), *Meeting the needs of African American women*. New Directions for Student Services, no. 104, pp. 79–94. San Francisco: Jossey-Bass.

Perna, L. W. (2005). Sex differences in faculty tenure and promotion: The contribution of family ties. *Research in Higher Education, 46*(3), 277–278.

Peterson, M. W., and Spencer, M. G. (1990). Understanding academic culture and climate. In W. G. Tierney (Ed.), *Assessing academic climates and cultures* (pp. 3–18). San Francisco: Jossey-Bass.

Pettigrew, T. F., and Martin, J. (1987). Shaping the organizational context for black American inclusion. *Journal of Social Issues, 43*(1), 41–78.

Ponterotto, J. G. (1990a). Affirmative action: Current status and future needs. In J. G. Ponterotto, D. E. Lewis, and R. Bullington (Eds.), *Affirmative action on campus* (pp. 5–16). San Francisco: Jossey-Bass.

Ponterotto, J. G. (1990b). Racial/ethnic minority and women administrators and faculty in higher education: A status report. In J. G. Ponterotto, D. E. Lewis, and R. Bullington (Eds.), *Affirmative action on campus* (pp. 61–72). San Francisco: Jossey-Bass.

Post, R., and Rogin, M. (Eds.). (1998). *Race and representation: Affirmative action*. New York: Zone Books.

Prilleltensky, I. (1994). The morals and politics of psychology: Psychological discourse and the status quo. Albany: State University of New York Press.

Prilleltensky, I., and Gonick, L. S. (1994). The discourse of oppression in the social sciences: Past, present, and future. In E. J. Trickett, R. J. Watts, and D. Birman (Eds.), *Human diversity: Perspectives on people in context* (pp. 145–177). San Francisco: Jossey-Bass.

Ragins, B. R. (1995). Diversity, power, and mentorship in organizations: A cultural, structural, and behavioral perspective. In M. M. Chemers, S. Oskamp, and M. Costanzo (Eds.), *Diversity in organizations: New perspectives for a changing workplace* (pp. 91–132). Thousand Oaks, CA: Sage.

Rai, K. B., and Critzer, J. W. (2000). *Affirmative action and the university: Race, ethnicity, and gender in higher education employment.* Lincoln: University of Nebraska Press.

Razack, S. R. (1998). *Looking white people in the eye: Gender, race, and culture in courtrooms and classrooms.* Toronto, Ontario: University of Toronto Press.

Reinharz, S. (1994). Toward an ethnography of "voice" and "silence." In E. J. Trickett, R. J. Watts, and D. Birman (Eds.), *Human diversity: Perspectives on people in context* (pp. 178–200). San Francisco: Jossey-Bass.

Roberts, R. K., Swanson, N. G., and Murphy, L. R. (2004). Discrimination and occupational mental health. *Journal of Mental Health, 13*(2), 129–142.

Roberts, S. K. (1999). *In the path of virtue: The African American moral tradition.* Cleveland, OH: Pilgrim Press.

Rodriguez, N. M. (1998). Employing the content of whiteness: Toward an understanding of the relations between whiteness and pedagogy. In J. L. Kincheloe, S. R. Steinberg, N. M. Rodriguez, and R. E. Chennault (Eds.), *White reign: Deploying whiteness in America* (pp. 31–62). New York: St. Martin's Press.

Ropers-Huilman, B. (Ed.). (2003). *Gendered futures in higher education: Critical perspectives for change.* Albany: State University of New York Press.

Ruggiero, K. M., and Taylor, D. M. (1997). Why minority group members perceive or do not perceive the discrimination that confronts them: The role of self-esteem and perceived control. *Journal of Personality and Social Psychology, 72*(2), 373–389.

Sackett, P. R., DuBois, C.L.Z., and Noe, A. W. (1991). Tokenism in performance evaluation: The effects of work group representation on male-female and white-black differences in performance ratings. *Journal of Applied Psychology, 76*(2), 263–267.

Saez-Santiago, E., and Bernal, G. (2003). Depression in ethnic minorities: Latinos and Latinas, African Americans, Asian Americans, and Native Americans. In G. Bernal, J. E. Trimble, A. K. Burlew, and F. T. Leong (Eds.), *Handbook of racial and ethnic minority psychology* (pp. 377–400). Thousand Oaks, CA: Sage.

St. Jean, Y., and Feagin, J. R. (1998). *Double burden: Black women and everyday racism.* Armonk, NY: M. E. Sharpe.

Sanchez, J. I., and Brock, P. (1996). Outcomes of perceived discrimination among Hispanic employees: Is diversity management a luxury or a necessity? *Academy of Management Journal, 39*(3), 704–719.

Sands, R. G., Parson, A. L., and Duane, J. (1991). Faculty mentoring faculty in a public university. *Journal of Higher Education, 62*(2), 174–193.

Sapolsky, R. M. (1992). *Stress, the aging brain, and the mechanisms of neuron death.* Cambridge, MA: MIT Press.

Sapolsky, R. M. (1998). *Why zebras don't get ulcers: An updated guide to stress, stress-related diseases and coping* (2nd ed.). New York: W. H. Freeman.

Schaefer, N. (2002). The big snooze: How college trustees are failing their universities. *American Enterprise, 13*(6), 32–37.

Schein, E. H. (1992). *Organizational culture and leadership.* San Francisco: Jossey-Bass.

Scheurich, J. J., and Young, M. D. (2002). White racism among white faculty: From critical understanding to antiracist activism. In W. A. Smith, P. G. Altbach, and K. Lomotey (Eds.), *The racial crisis in American higher education: Continuing challenges for the twenty-first century* (pp. 221–242). Albany: State University of New York Press.

Schwindt, L., Hall, K., and Davis, R. H. (1998). Affirmative action in action: A case study of faculty recruitment at one major land grant university. *NWSA Journal, 10*(3), 73–100.

Scott, J. W. (1996). Defending the tradition of shared governance. *Chronicle of Higher Education, 42*(48), B1–B3.

Senge, P. (2000a). The academy as learning community: Contradiction in terms or realizable future? In A. F. Lucas (Ed.), *Leading academic change: Essential roles for department chairs* (pp. 275–300). San Francisco: Jossey-Bass.

Senge, P. (2000b). The puzzles and paradoxes of how living companies create wealth: Why single-valued objective functions are not quite enough. In M. Beer and N. Nohria (Eds.), *Breaking the code of change* (pp. 59–81). Boston: Harvard Business School Press.

Smith, D. G. (1995). Organizational implications of diversity in higher education. In M. M. Chemers, S. Oskamp, and M. Costanzo (Eds.), *Diversity in organizations: New perspectives for a changing workplace* (pp. 220–244). Thousand Oaks, CA: Sage.

Smith, D. G., and others. (2000). *A diversity research agenda: Campus diversity initiatives.* Washington, DC: Association of American Colleges and Universities.

Smith, D. G., and Parker, S. (2005). Organizational learning: A tool for diversity and institutional effectiveness. In A. J. Kezar (Ed.), *Organizational learning in higher education* (pp. 113–126). San Francisco: Jossey-Bass.

Smith, D. G., Turner, C. S., Osei-Kofi, N., and Richards, S. (2004). Interrupting the usual: Successful strategies for hiring diverse faculty. *Journal of Higher Education, 75*(2), 133–160.

Smith, D. G., and Wolf-Wendel, L. (2005). *The challenge of diversity: Involvement or alienation in the academy?* ASHE-ERIC Higher Education Report, Vol. 31, No. 1. (Rev. ed.). San Francisco: Jossey-Bass.

Smith, E., Anderson, J. L., and Lovrich, N. P. (1995). The multiple sources of workplace stress among land-grant university faculty. *Research in Higher Education, 36*(3), 261–282.

Smith, E., and Witt, S. L. (1996). A comparative study of occupational stress among African American and white university faculty: A research note. In C.S.V. Turner, M. Garcia, A. Nora, and L. I. Rendon (Eds.), *Racial and ethnic diversity in higher education* (pp. 381–389). Needham Heights, MA: Simon & Schuster.

Snipes, R. L., Oswald, S. L., and Caudill, S. B. (1998). Sex-role stereotyping, gender biases, and job selection: The use of ordinal logIT in analyzing Likert scale data. *Employee Responsibilities and Rights Journal, 11*(2), 81–97.

Spalter-Roth, R., and Erskine, W. (2005). Beyond the fear factor: Work/family policies in academia—resources or rewards? *Change, 37*(6), 18–25.

Steele, C. M. (1997). A threat in the air: How stereotypes shape intellectual identity and performance. *American Psychologist, 1*(6), 613–629.

Steinpreis, R. E., Anders, K. A., and Ritzke, D. (1999). The impact of gender on the review of the curricula vitae of job applicants and tenure candidates: A national empirical study. *Sex Roles, 41*(7/8), 509–528.

Tack, M. W., and Patitu, C. L. (1992). *Faculty job satisfaction: Women and minorities in peril.* ASHE-ERIC Higher Education Report, No. 4. Washington, DC: School of Education and Human Development, George Washington University.

Tenure in a chilly climate. (1999). *PS: Political Science and Politics, 32*(1), 91–99.

Thomas, D. A. (2001). The truth about mentoring minorities: Race matters. *Harvard Business Review, 79*(4), 99–107.

Thomas, D. A., and Gabarro, J. J. (1999). *Breaking through: The making of minority executives in corporate America.* Boston: Harvard Business School Press.

Thomas, G. D., and Hollenshead, C. (2001). Resisting from the margins: The coping strategies of black women and other women of color faculty members at a research university. *Journal of Negro Education, 70*(3), 166–175.

Thomas, R. R., Jr. (1990). From affirmative action to affirming diversity. *Harvard Business Review, 90*(2), 107–117.

Thomas, R. R., Jr. (1991). *Beyond race and gender: Unleashing the power of your total work force by managing diversity.* New York: American Management Association.

Thomas, R. R., Jr. (1996). *Redefining diversity.* New York: American Management Association.

Thompson, C. J., and Dey, E. L. (1998). Pushed to the margins: Sources of stress for African American college and university faculty. *Journal of Higher Education, 69*(3), 324–345.

Tierney, W. G. (2002). Tenure and academic freedom in the academy: Historical parameters and new challenges. In J. Cooper and D. D. Stevens (Eds.), *Tenure in the sacred grove: Issues and strategies for women and minority faculty* (pp. 57–68). Albany: State University of New York Press.

Tierney, W. G., and Bensimon, E. M. (1996). *Promotion and tenure: Community and socialization in academe.* Albany: State University of New York Press.

Tierney, W. G., and Rhoads, R. A. (1994). *Faculty socialization as cultural process: A mirror of institutional commitment.* ASHE-ERIC Higher Education Report, No. 6. Washington, DC: School of Education and Human Development, George Washington University.

Tillman, L. C. (2001). Mentoring African American faculty in predominantly white institutions. *Research in Higher Education, 42*(3), 295–325.

Toma, J. D., Dubrow, G., and Hartley, M. (2005). *The uses of institutional culture: Strengthening identification and building brand equity in higher education.* ASHE-ERIC Higher Education Report, Vol. 31, No. 3. San Francisco: Jossey-Bass.

Townsend, B. K., Newell, L. J., and Wiese, M. D. (1992). *Creating distinctiveness: Lessons from uncommon colleges and universities.* ASHE-ERIC Higher Education Report, No. 6. Washington, DC: School of Education and Human Development, George Washington University.

Trower, C. A., and Bleak, J. L. (2004). *Study of new scholars. Race: Statistical report [universities].* Retrieved July 7, 2006, from http://www.gse.havard.edu/~newscholars/newscholars/downloads/racereport.pdf.

Trower, C. A., and Chait, R. P. (2002). Faculty diversity: Too little for too long. *Harvard Magazine, 104*(4), 33–37+. Retrieved August 30, 2006, from http://www.harvardmagazine.com/on-line/030218.html.

Turner, C.S.V. (2002). Women of color in academe: Living with multiple marginality. *Journal of Higher Education, 73*(1), 74–93.

Turner, C.S.V., and Myers, S. L. (2000). *Faculty of color in academe: Bittersweet success.* Boston: Allyn & Bacon.

Turner, C.S.V., Myers, S. L., Samuel, L., and Creswell, J. W. (1999). Exploring underrepresentation: The case of faculty of color in the Midwest. *Journal of Higher Education, 70*(1), 27–45.

Ulrich, D. (1997). *Human resource champions.* Boston: Harvard Business School Press.

Ulrich, D., and Smallwood, N. (2004). Capitalizing on capabilities. *Harvard Business Review, 82*(6), 119–127.

University of Arizona. (2003). *Diversity action plan.* Retrieved June 12, 2006, from http://diversity.arizona.edu/pdf/Diversity_Action_Plan_2003–04.pdf.

University of Washington. (2004). *Diversity appraisal report.* Retrieved June 12, 2006, from http://depts.washington.edu/divinit/UW%20Diversity%20Appraisal%20revised.pdf.

U.S. Department of Education. (2003a). *2003 race and gender of administrative, executive, and managerial staff at public doctoral research universities.* Analysis by the American Council on Education. Washington, DC: National Center for Education Statistics, Integrated Postsecondary Education System.

U.S. Department of Education. (2003b). *2003 race and gender of full-time faculty at public doctoral research universities with tenure systems (percent within rank).* Analysis by the American Council on Education. Washington, DC: National Center for Education Statistics, Integrated Postsecondary Education System.

Valdata, P. (2005). The ticking of the biological and tenure clocks. *Diverse Issues in Higher Education, 22*(20), 34–37.

Valverde, L. A. (1998). Future strategies and actions: Creating multicultural higher education campuses. In L. A. Valverde and L. A. Castenell Jr. (Eds.), *The multicultural campus: Strategies for transforming higher education* (pp. 13–29). Walnut Creek, CA: AltaMira Press.

Van Ummersen, C. A. (2005). No talent left behind. *Change, 37*(6), 26–31.

Ward, K. (2003). *Faculty service roles and the scholarship of engagement.* ASHE-ERIC Higher Education Report, Vol. 29, No. 5. San Francisco: Jossey-Bass.

Ward, K., and Wolf-Wendel, L. E. (2004). Fear factor: How safe is it to make time for family? *Academe, 90*(6), 28–31.

Westhues, K. (Ed.). (2004). *Workplace mobbing in academe: Reports from twenty universities.* Lewiston, NY: Edwin Mellen Press.

White, J. S. (2005). Pipelines to pathways: New directions for improving the status of women on campus. *Liberal Education, 91*(1), 22–27.

Wilcox, J. R., and Ebbs, S. L. (1992). *The leadership compass: Values and ethics in higher education.* ASHE-ERIC Higher Education Report, No. 1. Washington, DC: School of Education and Human Development, George Washington University.

Williams, D. A., Berger, J. B., and McClendon, S. A. (2005). *Toward a model of inclusive excellence and change in postsecondary institutions.* Retrieved May 24, 2006, from http://www.aacu.org/inclusive_excellence/documents/Williams_et_al.pdf.

Williams, D. R., Yu, Y., Jackson, J. S., and Anderson, N. B. (1997). Racial differences in physical and mental health: Socioeconomic status, stress and discrimination. *American Journal of Health Psychology, 2*(3), 335–351.

Williams, P. (1991). *The alchemy of race and rights: Diary of a law professor.* Cambridge, MA: Harvard University Press.

Wilson, E. O. (1998). *Consilience: The unity of knowledge.* New York: Vintage Books.

Wilson, R. (2004). Women in higher education: Where the elite teach, it's still a man's world. *Chronicle of Higher Education, 51*(15), A8–A14. Retrieved June 20, 2006, from http://chronicle.com/weekly/v51/i15/15a00801.htm.

Winkler, J. A. (2000). Faculty reappointment, tenure, and promotion: Barriers for women. *Professional Geographer, 52*(4), 737–750.

Wirth, L. (2001). *Breaking through the glass ceiling: Women in management.* Geneva, Switzerland: International Labour Office.

Word, C. O., Zanna, M. P., and Cooper, J. (2000). The nonverbal mediation of self-fulfilling prophecies in interracial interaction. In C. Stangor (Ed.), *Stereotypes and prejudice: Essential readings* (pp. 226–233). Philadelphia: Psychology Press.

Wright, E. O., and Baxter, J. (2000). The glass ceiling hypothesis: A reply to critics. *Gender and Society, 14*(6), 814–821.

Wu, F. H. (1995). Neither black nor white: Asian Americans and affirmative action. *Boston College Third World Law Journal, 15*(2), 225–284.

Wylie, A. (1995). The contexts of activism on "climate" issues. In The Chilly Collective (Eds.), *Breaking anonymity: The chilly climate for women faculty* (pp. 29–60). Waterloo, Ontario: Wilfried Laurier University Press.

Yoder, J. D., Aniakudo, P., and Berendsen, L. (1996). Looking beyond gender: The effects of racial differences on tokenism perceptions of women. *Sex Roles: A Journal of Research, 35*(7), 389–400.

Young, I. P., and Fox, J. A. (2002). Asian, Hispanic, and Native American job candidates: Prescreened or screened within the selection process. *Educational Administration Quarterly, 38*(4), 530–554.

Young, S. (2003). Micro-inequities: The power of small. *Workforce Diversity Reader, 1*(1), 88–95.

Zapata, M. (1995). African-American appointments in higher education continue to favor men. *Journal of Blacks in Higher Education, 8*, 22–24.

Name Index

A

Aguirre, A., Jr., 6, 7, 22, 61, 62, 67, 68, 81, 87, 105
Alexander, L., 72
Allen, W., 21
Anders, K. A., 59
Anderson, J. L., 44
Anderson, E. L., 8, 9
Anderson, N. B., 24, 25
Aniakudo, P., 27
Antonio, A. L., 6, 87, 88
Arveson, P., 96
Astin, H. S., 10
Austin, A. E., 87

B

Baez, B., 84
Bashaw, C. T., 75
Basinger, J., 70
Baxter, J., 66
Beatty, R. W., 96
Becker, B. E., 96
Bell, L. A., 13, 15
Bensimon, E. M., 26, 80, 81
Berendsen, L., 27
Berger, J. B., 97
Bernal, G., 25
Blackburn, R. T., 76
Blakemore, J.E.O., 81
Boyer, E. L., 88
Bradburn, E. M., 70
Britt, R. R., 24
Brock, P., 44

Brockbank, W., 38
Broder, D. S., 104
Bronstein, P., 79, 80, 81, 88
Busenberg, B. E., 28

C

Caudill, S. B., 64
Centra, J. A., 85
Chait, R. P., 2, 87
Chandler, D. L., 80
Chang, M. J., 6
Chase, S. E., 17
Chong, Y., 3
Chun, E., 97
Clark, R., 24
Clark, V. R., 24
Clayton-Pedersen, A., 6, 21
Collins, P. H., 13, 15, 16
Cooper, J., 12, 57, 75, 80
Creswell, J. W., 33
Critzer, J. W., 2, 8, 9, 10
Crocker, J., 45
Crosby, F. J., 30, 35
Cross, E. Y., 44
Cross, T., 59
Curry, B. K., 81

D

Darlington, P.S.E., 17, 18
Davis, R. H., 78
de la Luz Reyes, M., 40
Deitch, E. A., 40, 45, 47
Des Jarlais, C. D., 12, 75, 83

Leatherman, C., 72
Ledford, G. E., Jr., 95
Levin, R., 7
Lewis, T. T., 24, 25
Lima, M., 7, 87
Lindholm, J. A., 37
Lindsay, B., 62, 73
Loden, M., 26, 31
Lovrich, N. P., 44

M

MacDermid, S., 101
Major, B., 45
Maple, S. A., 86
Marschke, R., 8, 12, 60
Martin, J., 65, 72
Martinez, R. O., 6, 7, 22, 61, 67, 68, 87, 105
Maxwell, W. J., 72
McCarty, C. E., 63
McClendon, S. A., 97
McDavis, R. J., 24
McDonough, P. M., 69, 79, 80
McKinney, K. D., 40
Mickelson, K. D., 40
Milem, J. F., 6, 10, 21
Minor, J. T., 68
Moore, W., Jr., 76, 77
Moreno, J. F., 5
Mulvaney, B. M., 17, 18
Murphy, L. R., 25
Musil, C. M., 6, 95
Myers, H. F., 24, 25, 35
Myers, S. L., 27, 33, 44, 61

N

Nagowski, M. P., 70, 71
Nakanishi, D. T., 85, 86
Nelson, D. J., 59
Newell, L. J., 6
Nidiffer, J., 75
Nielsen, J. M., 8, 12, 60
Niemann, Y. F., 27, 82, 83
Noe, A. W., 65
Norton, D., 96

O

O'Brien, E., 3
O'Connor, S. D., 34, 35
Olsen, D., 86
Osei-Kofi, N., 77
Oswald, S. L., 64

P

Parasuraman, S., 60
Parham, T. A., 24
Park, S. M., 12, 58, 88
Parker, 94, 95
Parker-Dominguez, T., 24, 25
Parson, A. L., 63, 64
Patitu, C. L., 58, 60, 61, 79
Perna, L. W., 10, 12, 58
Peterson, M. W., 38, 39
Pettigrew, T. F., 65
Pfeffer, J., 91
Ponterotto, J. G., 16, 100
Post, R., 34
Powell, L. F., 34
Prilleltensky, I., x, 4, 13, 14, 16, 18, 19, 30

R

Ragins, B. R., 39, 58, 61, 64, 76
Rai, K. B., 2, 8, 9, 10
Ramaley, J. A., 79
Rankin, P., 8, 12, 60
Razack, S. R., 13, 15, 16, 22
Rehnquist, Justice, 35
Reinharz, S., 22, 23
Rhoads, R. A., 79
Rice, R. E., 87
Richards, S., 77
Ritzke, D., 59
Roberts, R. K., 25
Roberts, S. K., 17
Rogers, D. C., 59
Rogin, M., 34
Roosevelt, F. D., 29
Ropers-Huilman, B., 38
Rosener, J. B., 26, 31
Ross, E., 84
Rowe, A., 36

Subject Index

A

Academic department chairs
    tenure process and, 79–80 workplace
      power and, 68–69
Academic Quality Improvement Project
    of the Higher Learning Commission
    of the North Central Association of
    Colleges and Schools, 95
Accommodating campus, 36
Accreditation process, 7, 71–72, 95
Administrative positions, 8–9
Affirmative action
    culture, climate, and, 37–38
    diversity and, 31–34
    effectiveness of, 27–28, 40–41
    historical development of, 28–30
    structural change through, 8–12
Ambiguous empowerment, 16–17
Annual affirmative action plan,
    2, 100
Attributional ambiguity, 45
Aversive racism, 48
Avoidance and social distance theory,
    47–48

B

Bakke, Regents v., 34
Barriers. *See* Organizational barriers
Boards of trustees, 69
Bollinger, Grutter v., 34, 35
Bullying, 40. *See also* Workplace
    mobbing

C

Civic preparation, 6
Civil Rights Act of 1964, 29
Columbia University, Weinstock v., 85
Consilience, 12–13
Core values, 105
Cultural audits, 96
Culture and climate
    role of, 21, 37–40
    tenure success and, 80–84

D

Discrimination, workplace
    dimensions of, 46–51
    self-esteem and, 51–53
    stress and, 23–25, 53–55, 103
Discrimination claims and tenure denial,
    84–86
Diversity
    affirmative action and, 31–34
    culture, climate, and, 37–40
    decentralization and, 72–73
    lip service to, 40–41
    stages in developing, 36–37
    Supreme Court decisions and, 34–36
Diversity assessment, conceptual
    approach to, 94–96
Diversity scorecard, 96–100

E

EEOC, University of Pennsylvania v., 85
Engagement, 4–5

About the Authors

Alvin Evans is associate vice president for human resources at Kent State University, a doctoral extensive university with eight campuses. He has more than twenty years of experience in human resources and served as director of personnel for the Cleveland School District before coming to Kent State. At Kent State he oversees a broad range of functions, including recruitment and staffing, labor relations, and benefits. His educational background includes doctoral studies in history, government, and international studies at the University of South Carolina.

Edna Breinig Chun is vice president for human resources and equity at Broward Community College, a large urban institution in Fort Lauderdale, Florida, with three main campus locations and five centers serving sixty thousand students. She has two decades of experience in human resource leadership in higher education, including public research universities in California, Oregon, and Ohio. She is a frequent presenter on topics related to diversity at national and regional conferences. Chun received her Doctor of Music degree from Indiana University.

About the ASHE Higher Education Report Series

Since 1983, the ASHE (formerly ASHE-ERIC) Higher Education Report Series has been providing researchers, scholars, and practitioners with timely and substantive information on the critical issues facing higher education. Each monograph presents a definitive analysis of a higher education problem or issue, based on a thorough synthesis of significant literature and institutional experiences. Topics range from planning to diversity and multiculturalism, to performance indicators, to curricular innovations. The mission of the Series is to link the best of higher education research and practice to inform decision making and policy. The reports connect conventional wisdom with research and are designed to help busy individuals keep up with the higher education literature. Authors are scholars and practitioners in the academic community. Each report includes an executive summary, review of the pertinent literature, descriptions of effective educational practices, and a summary of key issues to keep in mind to improve educational policies and practice.

The Series is one of the most peer reviewed in higher education. A National Advisory Board made up of ASHE members reviews proposals. A National Review Board of ASHE scholars and practitioners reviews completed manuscripts. Six monographs are published each year and they are approximately 120 pages in length. The reports are widely disseminated through Jossey-Bass and John Wiley & Sons, and they are available online to subscribing institutions through Wiley InterScience (http://www.interscience.wiley.com).

Call for Proposals

The ASHE Higher Education Report Series is actively looking for proposals. We encourage you to contact one of the editors, Dr. Kelly Ward (kaward@wsu.edu) or Dr. Lisa Wolf-Wendel (lwolf@ku.edu), with your ideas.

Recent Titles